Psalms
and Proverbs

Amplified Version

Printed by Nedley Publishing, 2010, 2015, 2017

To order additional copies, call or write to:
      Nedley Publishing
      P. O. Box 1565
      Ardmore, OK 73402
      (888) 778-4445
      (580) 226-8007 (International)
      info@drnedley.com
      www.nedleyhealthsolutions.com

ISBN-13: 978-1-61584-301-5

Psalms

PSALM 1

[1]BLESSED (HAPPY, fortunate, prosperous, and enviable) is the man who walks and lives not in the counsel of the ungodly [following their advice, their plans and purposes], nor stands [submissive and inactive] in the path where sinners walk, nor sits down [to relax and rest] where the scornful [and the mockers] gather.

[2]But his delight and desire are in the law of the Lord, and on His law (the precepts, the instructions, the teachings of God) he habitually meditates (ponders and studies) by day and by night.

[3]And he shall be like a tree firmly planted [and tended] by the streams of water, ready to bring forth its fruit in its season; its leaf also shall not fade or wither; and everything he does shall prosper [and come to maturity].

[4]Not so the wicked [those disobedient and living without God are not so]. But they are like the chaff [worthless, dead, without substance] which the wind drives away.

[5]Therefore the wicked [those disobedient and living without God] shall not stand [justified] in the judgment, nor sinners in the congregation of the righteous [those who are upright and in right standing with God].

[6]For the Lord knows and is fully acquainted with the way of the righteous, but the way of the ungodly [those living outside God's will] shall perish (end in ruin and come to nought).

PSALM 2

[1]WHY DO the nations assemble with commotion [uproar and confusion of voices], and why do the people imagine (meditate upon and devise) an empty scheme?

[2]The kings of the earth take their places; the rulers take counsel together against the Lord and His Anointed One (the Messiah, the Christ). They say,

[3]Let us break Their bands [of restraint] asunder and cast Their cords [of control] from us.

[4]He Who sits in the heavens laughs; the Lord has them in derision [and in supreme contempt He mocks them].

[5]He speaks to them in His deep anger and troubles (terrifies and confounds) them in His displeasure and fury, saying,

⁶Yet have I anointed My King [firmly] on My holy hill of Zion.

⁷I will declare the decree of the Lord: He said to Me, You are My Son; this day [I declare] I have begotten You.

⁸Ask of Me, and I will give You the nations as Your inheritance, and the uttermost parts of the earth as Your possession.

⁹You shall break them with a rod of iron; You shall dash them in pieces like potters' ware.

¹⁰Now therefore, O you kings, act wisely; be instructed and warned, O you rulers of the earth.

¹¹Serve the Lord with reverent awe and worshipful fear; rejoice and be in high spirits with trembling [lest you displease Him].

¹²Kiss the Son [pay homage to Him in purity], lest He be angry and you perish in the way, for soon shall His wrath be kindled. O blessed (happy, fortunate, and to be envied) are all those who seek refuge and put their trust in Him!

PSALM 3

A Psalm of David. When he fled from Absalom his son.

¹LORD, HOW they are increased who trouble me! Many are they who rise up against me.

²Many are saying of me, There is no help for him in God. Selah [pause, and calmly think of that]!

³But You, O Lord, are a shield for me, my glory, and the lifter of my head.

⁴With my voice I cry to the Lord, and He hears and answers me out of His holy hill. Selah [pause, and calmly think of that]!

⁵I lay down and slept; I wakened again, for the Lord sustains me.

⁶I will not be afraid of ten thousands of people who have set themselves against me round about.

⁷Arise, O Lord; save me, O my God! For You have struck all my enemies on the cheek; You have broken the teeth of the ungodly.

⁸Salvation belongs to the Lord; May Your blessing be upon Your people. Selah [pause, and calmly think of that]!

PSALM 4

To the Chief Musician; on stringed instruments.
A Psalm of David.

¹ANSWER ME when I call, O God of my righteousness (uprightness, justice, and right standing with You)! You have freed me when I was hemmed in and enlarged me when I was in distress; have mercy upon me and hear my prayer.

²O you sons of men, how long will you turn my honor and glory into shame? How long will you love vanity and futility and seek after lies? Selah [pause, and calmly think of that]!

³But know that the Lord has set apart for Himself [and given distinction to] him who is godly [the man of loving-kindness]. The Lord listens and heeds when I call to Him.

⁴Be angry [or stand in awe] and sin not; commune with your own hearts upon your beds and be silent (sorry for the things you say in your hearts). Selah [pause, and calmly think of that]!

⁵Offer just and right sacrifices; trust (lean on and be confident) in the Lord.

⁶Many say, Oh, that we might see some good! Lift up the light of Your countenance upon us, O Lord.

⁷You have put more joy and rejoicing in my heart than [they know] when their wheat and new wine have yielded abundantly.

⁸In peace I will both lie down and sleep, for You, Lord, alone make me dwell in safety and confident trust.

PSALM 5

To the Chief Musician; on wind instruments.
A Psalm of David.

¹LISTEN TO my words, O Lord, give heed to my sighing and groaning.

²Hear the sound of my cry, my King and my God, for to You do I pray.

³In the morning You hear my voice, O Lord; in the morning I prepare [a prayer, a sacrifice] for You and watch and wait [for You to speak to my heart].

⁴For You are not a God Who takes pleasure in wickedness; neither will the evil [man] so much as dwell [temporarily] with You.

⁵Boasters can have no standing in Your sight; You abhor all evildoers.

⁶You will destroy those who speak lies; the Lord abhors [and rejects] the bloodthirsty and deceitful man.

⁷But as for me, I will enter Your house through the abundance of Your steadfast love and mercy; I will worship toward and at Your holy temple in reverent fear and awe of You.

⁸Lead me, O Lord, in Your righteousness because of my enemies; make Your way level (straight and right) before my face.

⁹For there is nothing trustworthy or steadfast or truthful in their talk; their heart is destruction [or a destructive chasm, a yawning gulf]; their throat is an open sepulcher; they flatter and make smooth with their tongue.

¹⁰Hold them guilty, O God; let them fall by their own designs and counsels; cast them out because of the multitude of their transgressions, for they have rebelled against You.

¹¹But let all those who take refuge and put their trust in You rejoice; let them ever sing and shout for joy, because You make a covering over them and defend them; let those also who love Your name be joyful in You and be in high spirits.

¹²For You, Lord, will bless the [uncompromisingly] righteous [him who is upright and in right standing with You]; as with a shield You will surround him with goodwill (pleasure and favor).

PSALM 6

To the Chief Musician; on stringed instruments, set [possibly] an octave below. A Psalm of David.

¹O LORD, rebuke me not in Your anger nor discipline and chasten me in Your hot displeasure.

²Have mercy on me and be gracious to me, O Lord, for I am weak (faint and withered away); O Lord, heal me, for my bones are troubled.

³My [inner] self [as well as my body] is also exceedingly disturbed and troubled. But You, O Lord, how long [until You return and speak peace to me]?

⁴Return [to my relief], O Lord, deliver my life; save me for the sake of Your steadfast love and mercy.

⁵For in death there is no remembrance of You; in Sheol (the place of the dead) who will give You thanks?

⁶I am weary with my groaning; all night I soak my pillow with tears, I drench my couch with my weeping.

⁷My eye grows dim because of grief; it grows old because of all my enemies.

⁸Depart from me, all you workers of iniquity, for the Lord has heard the voice of my weeping.

⁹The Lord has heard my supplication; the Lord receives my prayer.

¹⁰Let all my enemies be ashamed and sorely troubled; let them turn back and be put to shame suddenly.

PSALM 7

An Ode of David, [probably] in a wild, irregular,
enthusiastic strain, which he sang to the Lord concerning the words
of Cush, a Benjamite.

¹O LORD my God, in You I take refuge and put my trust; save me from all those who pursue and persecute me, and deliver me,

²Lest my foe tear my life [from my body] like a lion, dragging me away while there is none to deliver.

³O Lord my God, if I have done this, if there is wrong in my hands,

⁴If I have paid back with evil him who was at peace with me or without cause have robbed him who was my enemy,

⁵Let the enemy pursue my life and take it; yes, let him trample my life to the ground and lay my honor in the dust. Selah [pause, and calmly think of that]!

⁶Arise, O Lord, in Your anger; lift up Yourself against the rage of my enemies; and awake [and stir up] for me the justice and vindication [that] You have commanded.

⁷Let the assembly of the peoples be gathered about You, and return on high over them.

⁸The Lord judges the people; judge me, O Lord, and do me justice according to my righteousness [my rightness, justice, and right standing with You] and according to the integrity that is in me.

⁹Oh, let the wickedness of the wicked come to an end, but establish the [uncompromisingly] righteous [those upright and in harmony with You]; for You, Who try the hearts and emotions and thinking powers, are a righteous God.

[10]My defense and shield depend on God, Who saves the upright in heart.

[11]God is a righteous Judge, yes, a God Who is indignant every day.

[12]If a man does not turn and repent, [God] will whet His sword; He has strung and bent His [huge] bow and made it ready [by treading it with His foot].

[13]He has also prepared for him deadly weapons; He makes His arrows fiery shafts.

[14]Behold, [the wicked man] conceives iniquity and is pregnant with mischief and gives birth to lies.

[15]He made a pit and hollowed it out and has fallen into the hole which he made [before the trap was completed].

[16]His mischief shall fall back in return upon his own head, and his violence come down [with the loose dirt] upon his own scalp.

[17]I will give to the Lord the thanks due to His rightness and justice, and I will sing praise to the name of the Lord Most High.

PSALM 8

To the Chief Musician; set to a Philistine lute, or [possibly] to a particular Hittite tune. A Psalm of David.

[1]O LORD, our Lord, how excellent is Your name in all the earth! You have set Your glory on [or above] the heavens.

[2]Out of the mouths of babes and unweaned infants You have established strength because of Your foes, that You might silence the enemy and the avenger.

[3]When I view and consider Your heavens, the work of Your fingers, the moon and the stars, which You have ordained and established,

[4]What is man that You are mindful of him, and the son of [earthborn] man that You care for him?

[5]Yet You have made him but a little lower than God [or heavenly beings], and You have crowned him with glory and honor.

[6]You made him to have dominion over the works of Your hands; You have put all things under his feet:

[7]All sheep and oxen, yes, and the beasts of the field,

[8]The birds of the air, and the fish of the sea, and whatever passes along the paths of the seas.

[9]O Lord, our Lord, how excellent (majestic and glorious) is Your name in all the earth!

PSALM 9

To the Chief Musician; set for [possibly] soprano voices. A Psalm of David.

¹I WILL praise You, O Lord, with my whole heart; I will show forth (recount and tell aloud) all Your marvelous works and wonderful deeds!

²I will rejoice in You and be in high spirits; I will sing praise to Your name, O Most High!

³When my enemies turned back, they stumbled and perished before You.

⁴For You have maintained my right and my cause; You sat on the throne judging righteously.

⁵You have rebuked the nations, You have destroyed the wicked; You have blotted out their name forever and ever.

⁶The enemy have been cut off and have vanished in everlasting ruins, You have plucked up and overthrown their cities; the very memory of them has perished and vanished.

⁷But the Lord shall remain and continue forever; He has prepared and established His throne for judgment.

⁸And He will judge the world in righteousness (rightness and equity); He will minister justice to the peoples in uprightness.

⁹The Lord also will be a refuge and a high tower for the oppressed, a refuge and a stronghold in times of trouble (high cost, destitution, and desperation).

¹⁰And they who know Your name [who have experience and acquaintance with Your mercy] will lean on and confidently put their trust in You, for You, Lord, have not forsaken those who seek (inquire of and for) You [on the authority of God's Word and the right of their necessity].

¹¹Sing praises to the Lord, Who dwells in Zion! Declare among the peoples His doings!

¹²For He Who avenges the blood [of His people shed unjustly] remembers them; He does not forget the cry of the afflicted (the poor and the humble).

¹³Have mercy upon me and be gracious to me, O Lord; consider how I am afflicted by those who hate me, You Who lift me up from the gates of death,

¹⁴That I may show forth (recount and tell aloud) all Your praises! In the gates of the Daughter of Zion I will rejoice in Your salvation and Your saving help.

¹⁵The nations have sunk down in the pit that they made; in the net which they hid is their own foot caught.

¹⁶The Lord has made Himself known; He executes judgment; the wicked are snared in the work of their own hands. Higgaion [meditation]. Selah [pause, and calmly think of that]!

¹⁷The wicked shall be turned back [headlong into premature death] into Sheol (the place of the departed spirits of the wicked), even all the nations that forget or are forgetful of God.

¹⁸For the needy shall not always be forgotten, and the expectation and hope of the meek and the poor shall not perish forever.

¹⁹Arise, O Lord! Let not man prevail; let the nations be judged before You.

²⁰Put them in fear [make them realize their frail nature], O Lord, that the nations may know themselves to be but men. Selah [pause, and calmly think of that]!

PSALM 10

¹WHY DO You stand afar off, O Lord? Why do You hide Yourself, [veiling Your eyes] in times of trouble (distress and desperation)?

²The wicked in pride and arrogance hotly pursue and persecute the poor; let them be taken in the schemes which they have devised.

³For the wicked man boasts (sings the praises) of his own heart's desire, and the one greedy for gain curses and spurns, yes, renounces and despises the Lord.

⁴The wicked one in the pride of his countenance will not seek, inquire for, and yearn for God; all his thoughts are that there is no God [so He never punishes].

⁵His ways are grievous [or persist] at all times; Your judgments [Lord] are far above and on high out of his sight [so he never thinks about them]; as for all his foes, he sniffs and sneers at them.

⁶He thinks in his heart, I shall not be moved; for throughout all generations I shall not come to want or be in adversity.

⁷His mouth is full of cursing, deceit, oppression (fraud); under his tongue are trouble and sin (mischief and iniquity).

[8]He sits in ambush in the villages; in hiding places he slays the innocent; he watches stealthily for the poor (helpless and unfortunate).

[9]He lurks in secret places like a lion in his thicket; he lies in wait that he may seize the poor (the helpless and the unfortunate); he seizes the poor when he draws him into his net.

[10][The prey] is crushed, sinks down; and the helpless falls by his mighty [claws].

[11][The foe] thinks in his heart, God has quite forgotten; He has hidden His face; He will never see [my deed].

[12]Arise, O Lord! O God, lift up Your hand; forget not the humble [patient and crushed].

[13]Why does the wicked [man] condemn (spurn and renounce) God? Why has he thought in his heart, You will not call to account?

[14]You have seen it; yes, You note trouble and grief (vexation) to requite it with Your hand. The unfortunate commits himself to You; You are the helper of the fatherless.

[15]Break the arm of the wicked man; and as for the evil man, search out his wickedness until You find no more.

[16]The Lord is King forever and ever; the nations will perish out of His land.

[17]O Lord, You have heard the desire and the longing of the humble and oppressed; You will prepare and strengthen and direct their hearts, You will cause Your ear to hear,

[18]To do justice to the fatherless and the oppressed, so that man, who is of the earth, may not terrify them any more.

PSALM 11

To the Chief Musician or Choir Leader.
[A Psalm] of David.

[1]IN THE Lord I take refuge [and put my trust]; how can you say to me, Flee like a bird to your mountain?

[2]For see, the wicked are bending the bow; they make ready their arrow upon the string, that they [furtively] in darkness may shoot at the upright in heart.

[3]If the foundations are destroyed, what can the [unyieldingly] righteous do, or what has He [the Righteous One] wrought or accomplished?

⁴The Lord is in His holy temple; the Lord's throne is in heaven. His eyes behold; His eyelids test and prove the children of men.

⁵The Lord tests and proves the [unyieldingly] righteous, but His soul abhors the wicked and him who loves violence.

⁶Upon the wicked He will rain quick burning coals or snares; fire, brimstone, and a [dreadful] scorching wind shall be the portion of their cup.

⁷For the Lord is [rigidly] righteous, He loves righteous deeds; the upright shall behold His face, or He beholds the upright.

PSALM 12

To the Chief Musician; set [possibly] an octave below.
A Psalm of David.

¹HELP, LORD! For principled and godly people are here no more; faithfulness and the faithful vanish from among the sons of men.

²To his neighbor each one speaks words without use or worth or truth; with flattering lips and double heart [deceitfully] they speak.

³May the Lord cut off all flattering lips and the tongues that speak proud boasting,

⁴Those who say, With our tongues we prevail; our lips are our own [to command at our will]--who is lord and master over us?

⁵Now will I arise, says the Lord, because the poor are oppressed, because of the groans of the needy; I will set him in safety and in the salvation for which he pants.

⁶The words and promises of the Lord are pure words, like silver refined in an earthen furnace, purified seven times over.

⁷You will keep them and preserve them, O Lord; You will guard and keep us from this [evil] generation forever.

⁸The wicked walk or prowl about on every side, as vileness is exalted [and baseness is rated high] among the sons of men.

PSALM 13

To the Chief Musician. A Psalm of David.

¹HOW LONG will You forget me, O Lord? Forever? How long will You hide Your face from me?

²How long must I lay up cares within me and have sorrow in my heart day after day? How long shall my enemy exalt himself over me?

³Consider and answer me, O Lord my God; lighten the eyes [of my faith to behold Your face in the pitchlike darkness], lest I sleep the sleep of death,

⁴Lest my enemy say, I have prevailed over him, and those that trouble me rejoice when I am shaken.

⁵But I have trusted, leaned on, and been confident in Your mercy and loving-kindness; my heart shall rejoice and be in high spirits in Your salvation.

⁶I will sing to the Lord, because He has dealt bountifully with me.

PSALM 14
To the Chief Musician. [A Psalm] of David.

¹THE [empty-headed] fool has said in his heart, There is no God. They are corrupt, they have done abominable deeds; there is none that does good or right.

²The Lord looked down from heaven upon the children of men to see if there were any who understood, dealt wisely, and sought after God, inquiring for and of Him and requiring Him [of vital necessity].

³They are all gone aside, they have all together become filthy; there is none that does good or right, no, not one.

⁴Have all the workers of iniquity no knowledge, who eat up my people as they eat bread and who do not call on the Lord?

⁵There they shall be in great fear [literally--dreading a dread], for God is with the generation of the [uncompromisingly] righteous (those upright and in right standing with Him).

⁶You [evildoers] would put to shame and confound the plans of the poor and patient, but the Lord is his safe refuge.

⁷Oh, that the salvation of Israel would come out of Zion! When the Lord shall restore the fortunes of His people, then Jacob shall rejoice and Israel shall be glad.

PSALM 15
A Psalm of David.

¹LORD, WHO shall dwell [temporarily] in Your tabernacle? Who shall dwell [permanently] on Your holy hill?

²He who walks and lives uprightly and blamelessly, who works rightness and justice and speaks and thinks the truth in his heart,

³He who does not slander with his tongue, nor does evil to his friend, nor takes up a reproach against his neighbor;

⁴In whose eyes a vile person is despised, but he who honors those who fear the Lord (who revere and worship Him); who swears to his own hurt and does not change;

⁵[He who] does not put out his money for interest [to one of his own people] and who will not take a bribe against the innocent. He who does these things shall never be moved.

PSALM 16
A Poem of David; [probably] intended to record memorable thoughts.

¹KEEP and protect me, O God, for in You I have found refuge, and in You do I put my trust and hide myself.

²I say to the Lord, You are my Lord; I have no good beside or beyond You.

³As for the godly (the saints) who are in the land, they are the excellent, the noble, and the glorious, in whom is all my delight.

⁴Their sorrows shall be multiplied who choose another god; their drink offerings of blood will I not offer or take their names upon my lips.

⁵The Lord is my chosen and assigned portion, my cup; You hold and maintain my lot.

⁶The lines have fallen for me in pleasant places; yes, I have a good heritage.

⁷I will bless the Lord, Who has given me counsel; yes, my heart instructs me in the night seasons.

⁸I have set the Lord continually before me; because He is at my right hand, I shall not be moved.

⁹Therefore my heart is glad and my glory [my inner self] rejoices; my body too shall rest and confidently dwell in safety,

[10]For You will not abandon me to Sheol (the place of the dead), neither will You suffer Your holy one [Holy One] to see corruption.

[11]You will show me the path of life; in Your presence is fullness of joy, at Your right hand there are pleasures forevermore.

PSALM 17

A Prayer of David.

[1]HEAR THE right (my righteous cause), O Lord; listen to my shrill, piercing cry! Give ear to my prayer, that comes from unfeigned and guileless lips.

[2]Let my sentence of vindication come from You! May Your eyes behold the things that are just and upright.

[3]You have proved my heart; You have visited me in the night; You have tried me and find nothing [no evil purpose in me]; I have purposed that my mouth shall not transgress.

[4]Concerning the works of men, by the word of Your lips I have avoided the ways of the violent (the paths of the destroyer).

[5]My steps have held closely to Your paths [to the tracks of the One Who has gone on before]; my feet have not slipped.

[6]I have called upon You, O God, for You will hear me; incline Your ear to me and hear my speech.

[7]Show Your marvelous loving-kindness, O You Who save by Your right hand those who trust and take refuge in You from those who rise up against them.

[8]Keep and guard me as the pupil of Your eye; hide me in the shadow of Your wings

[9]From the wicked who despoil and oppress me, my deadly adversaries who surround me.

[10]They are enclosed in their own prosperity and have shut up their hearts to pity; with their mouths they make exorbitant claims and proudly and arrogantly speak.

[11]They track us down in each step we take; now they surround us; they set their eyes to cast us to the ground,

[12]Like a lion greedy and eager to tear his prey, and as a young lion lurking in hidden places.

[13]Arise, O Lord! Confront and forestall them, cast them down! Deliver my life from the wicked by Your sword,

¹⁴From men by Your hand, O Lord, from men of this world [these poor moths of the night] whose portion in life is idle and vain. Their bellies are filled with Your hidden treasure; their children are satiated, and they leave the rest [of their] wealth to their babes.

¹⁵As for me, I will continue beholding Your face in righteousness (justice, and right standing with You); I shall be fully satisfied, when I awake [to find myself] beholding Your form [having communion with You].

PSALM 18

To the Chief Musician. [A Psalm] of David the servant of the Lord, who spoke the words of this song to the Lord on the day when the Lord delivered him from the hand of all his enemies and from the hand of Saul. And he said:

¹I LOVE You fervently and devotedly, O Lord, my Strength.

²The Lord is my Rock, my Fortress, and my Deliverer; my God, my keen and firm Strength in Whom I will trust and take refuge, my Shield, and the Horn of my salvation, my High Tower.

³I will call upon the Lord, Who is to be praised; so shall I be saved from my enemies.

⁴The cords or bands of death surrounded me, and the streams of ungodliness and the torrents of ruin terrified me.

⁵The cords of Sheol (the place of the dead) surrounded me; the snares of death confronted and came upon me.

⁶In my distress [when seemingly closed in] I called upon the Lord and cried to my God; He heard my voice out of His temple (heavenly dwelling place), and my cry came before Him, into His [very] ears.

⁷Then the earth quaked and rocked, the foundations also of the mountains trembled; they moved and were shaken because He was indignant and angry.

⁸There went up smoke from His nostrils; and lightning out of His mouth devoured; coals were kindled by it.

⁹He bowed the heavens also and came down; and thick darkness was under His feet.

¹⁰And He rode upon a cherub [a storm] and flew [swiftly]; yes, He sped on with the wings of the wind.

¹¹He made darkness His secret hiding place; as His pavilion (His canopy) round about Him were dark waters and thick clouds of the skies.

¹²Out of the brightness before Him there broke forth through His thick clouds hailstones and coals of fire.

¹³The Lord also thundered from the heavens, and the Most High uttered His voice, amid hailstones and coals of fire.

¹⁴And He sent out His arrows and scattered them; and He flashed forth lightnings and put them to rout.

¹⁵Then the beds of the sea appeared and the foundations of the world were laid bare at Your rebuke, O Lord, at the blast of the breath of Your nostrils.

¹⁶He reached from on high, He took me; He drew me out of many waters.

¹⁷He delivered me from my strong enemy and from those who hated and abhorred me, for they were too strong for me.

¹⁸They confronted and came upon me in the day of my calamity, but the Lord was my stay and support.

¹⁹He brought me forth also into a large place; He was delivering me because He was pleased with me and delighted in me.

²⁰The Lord rewarded me according to my righteousness (my conscious integrity and sincerity with Him); according to the cleanness of my hands has He recompensed me.

²¹For I have kept the ways of the Lord and have not wickedly departed from my God.

²²For all His ordinances were before me, and I put not away His statutes from me.

²³I was upright before Him and blameless with Him, ever [on guard] to keep myself free from my sin and guilt.

²⁴Therefore has the Lord recompensed me according to my righteousness (my uprightness and right standing with Him), according to the cleanness of my hands in His sight.

²⁵With the kind and merciful You will show Yourself kind and merciful, with an upright man You will show Yourself upright,

²⁶With the pure You will show Yourself pure, and with the perverse You will show Yourself contrary.

²⁷For You deliver an afflicted and humble people but will bring down those with haughty looks.

²⁸For You cause my lamp to be lighted and to shine; the Lord my God illumines my darkness.

²⁹For by You I can run through a troop, and by my God I can leap over a wall.

[30]As for God, His way is perfect! The word of the Lord is tested and tried; He is a shield to all those who take refuge and put their trust in Him.

[31]For who is God except the Lord? Or who is the Rock save our God,

[32]The God who girds me with strength and makes my way perfect?

[33]He makes my feet like hinds' feet [able to stand firmly or make progress on the dangerous heights of testing and trouble]; He sets me securely upon my high places.

[34]He teaches my hands to war, so that my arms can bend a bow of bronze.

[35]You have also given me the shield of Your salvation, and Your right hand has held me up; Your gentleness and condescension have made me great.

[36]You have given plenty of room for my steps under me, that my feet would not slip.

[37]I pursued my enemies and overtook them; neither did I turn again till they were consumed.

[38]I smote them so that they were not able to rise; they fell wounded under my feet.

[39]For You have girded me with strength for the battle; You have subdued under me and caused to bow down those who rose up against me.

[40]You have also made my enemies turn their backs to me, that I might cut off those who hate me.

[41]They cried [for help], but there was none to deliver--even unto the Lord, but He answered them not.

[42]Then I beat them small as the dust before the wind; I emptied them out as the dirt and mire of the streets.

[43]You have delivered me from the strivings of the people; You made me the head of the nations; a people I had not known served me.

[44]As soon as they heard of me, they obeyed me; foreigners submitted themselves cringingly and yielded feigned obedience to me.

[45]Foreigners lost heart and came trembling out of their caves or strongholds.

[46]The Lord lives! Blessed be my Rock; and let the God of my salvation be exalted,

⁴⁷The God Who avenges me and subdues peoples under me,

⁴⁸Who delivers me from my enemies; yes, You lift me up above those who rise up against me; You deliver me from the man of violence.

⁴⁹Therefore will I give thanks and extol You, O Lord, among the nations, and sing praises to Your name.

⁵⁰Great deliverances and triumphs gives He to His king; and He shows mercy and steadfast love to His anointed, to David and his offspring forever.

PSALM 19
To the Chief Musician. A Psalm of David.

¹THE HEAVENS declare the glory of God; and the firmament shows and proclaims His handiwork.

²Day after day pours forth speech, and night after night shows forth knowledge.

³There is no speech nor spoken word [from the stars]; their voice is not heard.

⁴Yet their voice [in evidence] goes out through all the earth, their sayings to the end of the world. Of the heavens has God made a tent for the sun,

⁵Which is as a bridegroom coming out of his chamber; and it rejoices as a strong man to run his course.

⁶Its going forth is from the end of the heavens, and its circuit to the ends of it; and nothing [yes, no one] is hidden from the heat of it.

⁷The law of the Lord is perfect, restoring the [whole] person; the testimony of the Lord is sure, making wise the simple.

⁸The precepts of the Lord are right, rejoicing the heart; the commandment of the Lord is pure and bright, enlightening the eyes.

⁹The [reverent] fear of the Lord is clean, enduring forever; the ordinances of the Lord are true and righteous altogether.

¹⁰More to be desired are they than gold, even than much fine gold; they are sweeter also than honey and drippings from the honeycomb.

¹¹Moreover, by them is Your servant warned (reminded and instructed); and in keeping them there is great reward.

¹²Who can discern his lapses and errors? Clear me from hidden [and unconscious] faults.

¹³Keep back Your servant also from presumptuous sins; let them not have dominion over me! Then shall I be blameless, and I shall be innocent and clear of great transgression.

¹⁴Let the words of my mouth and the meditation of my heart be acceptable in Your sight, O Lord, my [firm, impenetrable] Rock and my Redeemer.

PSALM 20

To the Chief Musician. A Psalm of David.

¹MAY THE Lord answer you in the day of trouble! May the name of the God of Jacob set you up on high [and defend you];

²Send you help from the sanctuary and support, refresh, and strengthen you from Zion;

³Remember all your offerings and accept your burnt sacrifice. Selah [pause, and think of that]!

⁴May He grant you according to your heart's desire and fulfill all your plans.

⁵We will [shout in] triumph at your salvation and victory, and in the name of our God we will set up our banners. May the Lord fulfill all your petitions.

⁶Now I know that the Lord saves His anointed; He will answer him from His holy heaven with the saving strength of His right hand.

⁷Some trust in and boast of chariots and some of horses, but we will trust in and boast of the name of the Lord our God.

⁸They are bowed down and fallen, but we are risen and stand upright.

⁹O Lord, give victory; let the King answer us when we call.

PSALM 21

To the Chief Musician. A Psalm of David.

¹THE KING [David] shall joy in Your strength, O Lord; and in Your salvation how greatly shall he rejoice!

²You have given him his heart's desire and have not withheld the request of his lips. Selah [pause, and think of that]!

³For You send blessings of good things to meet him; You set a crown of pure gold on his head.

⁴He asked life of You, and You gave it to him--long life forever and evermore.

⁵His glory is great because of Your aid; splendor and majesty You bestow upon him.

⁶For You make him to be blessed and a blessing forever; You make him exceedingly glad with the joy of Your presence.

⁷For the king trusts, relies on, and is confident in the Lord, and through the mercy and steadfast love of the Most High he will never be moved.

⁸Your hand shall find all Your enemies; Your right hand shall find all those who hate You.

⁹You will make them as if in a blazing oven in the time of Your anger; the Lord will swallow them up in His wrath, and the fire will utterly consume them.

¹⁰Their offspring You will destroy from the earth, and their sons from among the children of men.

¹¹For they planned evil against You; they conceived a mischievous plot which they are not able to perform.

¹²For You will make them turn their backs; You will aim Your bow [of divine justice] at their faces.

¹³Be exalted, Lord, in Your strength; we will sing and praise Your power.

PSALM 22

To the Chief Musician; set to [the tune of]
Aijeleth Hashshahar [the hind of the morning dawn].
A Psalm of David.

¹MY GOD, my God, why have You forsaken me? Why are You so far from helping me, and from the words of my groaning?

²O my God, I cry in the daytime, but You answer not; and by night I am not silent or find no rest.

³But You are holy, O You Who dwell in [the holy place where] the praises of Israel [are offered].

⁴Our fathers trusted in You; they trusted (leaned on, relied on You, and were confident) and You delivered them.

⁵They cried to You and were delivered; they trusted in, leaned on, and confidently relied on You, and were not ashamed or confounded or disappointed.

⁶But I am a worm, and no man; I am the scorn of men, and despised by the people.

⁷All who see me laugh at me and mock me; they shoot out the lip, they shake the head, saying,

⁸He trusted and rolled himself on the Lord, that He would deliver him. Let Him deliver him, seeing that He delights in him!

⁹Yet You are He Who took me out of the womb; You made me hope and trust when I was on my mother's breasts.

¹⁰I was cast upon You from my very birth; from my mother's womb You have been my God.

¹¹Be not far from me, for trouble is near and there is none to help.

¹²Many [foes like] bulls have surrounded me; strong bulls of Bashan have hedged me in.

¹³Against me they opened their mouths wide, like a ravening and roaring lion.

¹⁴I am poured out like water, and all my bones are out of joint. My heart is like wax; it is softened [with anguish] and melted down within me.

¹⁵My strength is dried up like a fragment of clay pottery; [with thirst] my tongue cleaves to my jaws; and You have brought me into the dust of death.

¹⁶For [like a pack of] dogs they have encompassed me; a company of evildoers has encircled me, they pierced my hands and my feet.

¹⁷I can count all my bones; [the evildoers] gaze at me.

¹⁸They part my clothing among them and cast lots for my raiment (a long, shirtlike garment, a seamless undertunic).

¹⁹But be not far from me, O Lord; O my Help, hasten to aid me!

²⁰Deliver my life from the sword, my dear life [my only one] from the power of the dog [the agent of execution].

²¹Save me from the lion's mouth; for You have answered me [kindly] from the horns of the wild oxen.

²²I will declare Your name to my brethren; in the midst of the congregation will I praise You.

²³You who fear (revere and worship) the Lord, praise Him! All you offspring of Jacob, glorify Him. Fear (revere and worship) Him, all you offspring of Israel.

²⁴For He has not despised or abhorred the affliction of the afflicted; neither has He hidden His face from him, but when he cried to Him, He heard.

[25]My praise shall be of You in the great congregation. I will pay to Him my vows [made in the time of trouble] before them who fear (revere and worship) Him.

[26]The poor and afflicted shall eat and be satisfied; they shall praise the Lord--they who [diligently] seek for, inquire of and for Him, and require Him [as their greatest need]. May your hearts be quickened now and forever!

[27]All the ends of the earth shall remember and turn to the Lord, and all the families of the nations shall bow down and worship before You,

[28]For the kingship and the kingdom are the Lord's, and He is the ruler over the nations.

[29]All the mighty ones upon earth shall eat [in thanksgiving] and worship; all they that go down to the dust shall bow before Him, even he who cannot keep himself alive.

[30]Posterity shall serve Him; they shall tell of the Lord to the next generation.

[31]They shall come and shall declare His righteousness to a people yet to be born--that He has done it [that it is finished]!

PSALM 23

A Psalm of David.

[1]THE LORD is my Shepherd [to feed, guide, and shield me], I shall not lack.

[2]He makes me lie down in [fresh, tender] green pastures; He leads me beside the still and restful waters.

[3]He refreshes and restores my life (myself); He leads me in the paths of righteousness [uprightness and right standing with Him--not for my earning it, but] for His name's sake.

[4]Yes, though I walk through the [deep, sunless] valley of the shadow of death, I will fear or dread no evil, for You are with me; Your rod [to protect] and Your staff [to guide], they comfort me.

[5]You prepare a table before me in the presence of my enemies. You anoint my head with oil; my [brimming] cup runs over.

[6]Surely or only goodness, mercy, and unfailing love shall follow me all the days of my life, and through the length of my days the house of the Lord [and His presence] shall be my dwelling place.

PSALM 24

A Psalm of David.

¹THE EARTH is the Lord's, and the fullness of it, the world and they who dwell in it.

²For He has founded it upon the seas and established it upon the currents and the rivers.

³Who shall go up into the mountain of the Lord? Or who shall stand in His Holy Place?

⁴He who has clean hands and a pure heart, who has not lifted himself up to falsehood or to what is false, nor sworn deceitfully.

⁵He shall receive blessing from the Lord and righteousness from the God of his salvation.

⁶This is the generation [description] of those who seek Him [who inquire of and for Him and of necessity require Him], who seek Your face, [O God of] Jacob. Selah [pause, and think of that]!

⁷Lift up your heads, O you gates; and be lifted up, you age-abiding doors, that the King of glory may come in.

⁸Who is the King of glory? The Lord strong and mighty, the Lord mighty in battle.

⁹Lift up your heads, O you gates; yes, lift them up, you age-abiding doors, that the King of glory may come in.

¹⁰Who is [He then] this King of glory? The Lord of hosts, He is the King of glory. Selah [pause, and think of that]!

PSALM 25

[A Psalm] of David.

¹UNTO YOU, O Lord, do I bring my life.

²O my God, I trust, lean on, rely on, and am confident in You. Let me not be put to shame or [my hope in You] be disappointed; let not my enemies triumph over me.

³Yes, let none who trust and wait hopefully and look for You be put to shame or be disappointed; let them be ashamed who forsake the right or deal treacherously without cause.

⁴Show me Your ways, O Lord; teach me Your paths.

⁵Guide me in Your truth and faithfulness and teach me, for You are the God of my salvation; for You [You only and altogether] do I wait [expectantly] all the day long.

⁶Remember, O Lord, Your tender mercy and loving-kindness; for they have been ever from of old.

⁷Remember not the sins (the lapses and frailties) of my youth or my transgressions; according to Your mercy and steadfast love remember me, for Your goodness' sake, O Lord.

⁸Good and upright is the Lord; therefore will He instruct sinners in [His] way.

⁹He leads the humble in what is right, and the humble He teaches His way.

¹⁰All the paths of the Lord are mercy and steadfast love, even truth and faithfulness are they for those who keep His covenant and His testimonies.

¹¹For Your name's sake, O Lord, pardon my iniquity and my guilt, for [they are] great.

¹²Who is the man who reverently fears and worships the Lord? Him shall He teach in the way that he should choose.

¹³He himself shall dwell at ease, and his offspring shall inherit the land.

¹⁴The secret [of the sweet, satisfying companionship] of the Lord have they who fear (revere and worship) Him, and He will show them His covenant and reveal to them its [deep, inner] meaning.

¹⁵My eyes are ever toward the Lord, for He will pluck my feet out of the net.

¹⁶[Lord] turn to me and be gracious to me, for I am lonely and afflicted.

¹⁷The troubles of my heart are multiplied; bring me out of my distresses.

¹⁸Behold my affliction and my pain and forgive all my sins [of thinking and doing].

¹⁹Consider my enemies, for they abound; they hate me with cruel hatred.

²⁰O keep me, Lord, and deliver me; let me not be ashamed or disappointed, for my trust and my refuge are in You.

²¹Let integrity and uprightness preserve me, for I wait for and expect You.

²²Redeem Israel, O God, out of all their troubles.

PSALM 26
[A Psalm] of David.

¹VINDICATE ME, O Lord, for I have walked in my integrity; I have [expectantly] trusted in, leaned on, and relied on the Lord without wavering and I shall not slide.

²Examine me, O Lord, and prove me; test my heart and my mind.

³For Your loving-kindness is before my eyes, and I have walked in Your truth [faithfully].

⁴I do not sit with false persons, nor fellowship with pretenders;

⁵I hate the company of evildoers and will not sit with the wicked.

⁶I will wash my hands in innocence, and go about Your altar, O Lord,

⁷That I may make the voice of thanksgiving heard and may tell of all Your wondrous works.

⁸Lord, I love the habitation of Your house, and the place where Your glory dwells.

⁹Gather me not with sinners and sweep me not away [with them], nor my life with bloodthirsty men,

¹⁰In whose hands is wickedness, and their right hands are full of bribes.

¹¹But as for me, I will walk in my integrity; redeem me and be merciful and gracious to me.

¹²My foot stands on an even place; in the congregations will I bless the Lord.

PSALM 27
[A Psalm] of David.

¹THE LORD is my Light and my Salvation--whom shall I fear or dread? The Lord is the Refuge and Stronghold of my life--of whom shall I be afraid?

²When the wicked, even my enemies and my foes, came upon me to eat up my flesh, they stumbled and fell.

³Though a host encamp against me, my heart shall not fear; though war arise against me, [even then] in this will I be confident.

⁴One thing have I asked of the Lord, that will I seek, inquire for, and [insistently] require: that I may dwell in the house of the Lord [in His presence] all the days of my life, to behold and gaze upon the beauty [the sweet attractiveness and the delightful loveliness] of the Lord and to meditate, consider, and inquire in His temple.

⁵For in the day of trouble He will hide me in His shelter; in the secret place of His tent will He hide me; He will set me high upon a rock.

⁶And now shall my head be lifted up above my enemies round about me; in His tent I will offer sacrifices and shouting of joy; I will sing, yes, I will sing praises to the Lord.

⁷Hear, O Lord, when I cry aloud; have mercy and be gracious to me and answer me!

⁸You have said, Seek My face [inquire for and require My presence as your vital need]. My heart says to You, Your face (Your presence), Lord, will I seek, inquire for, and require [of necessity and on the authority of Your Word].

⁹Hide not Your face from me; turn not Your servant away in anger, You Who have been my help! Cast me not off, neither forsake me, O God of my salvation!

¹⁰Although my father and my mother have forsaken me, yet the Lord will take me up [adopt me as His child].

¹¹Teach me Your way, O Lord, and lead me in a plain and even path because of my enemies [those who lie in wait for me].

¹²Give me not up to the will of my adversaries, for false witnesses have risen up against me; they breathe out cruelty and violence.

¹³[What, what would have become of me] had I not believed that I would see the Lord's goodness in the land of the living!

¹⁴Wait and hope for and expect the Lord; be brave and of good courage and let your heart be stout and enduring. Yes, wait for and hope for and expect the Lord.

PSALM 28
[A Psalm] of David.

¹UNTO YOU do I cry, O Lord my Rock, be not deaf and silent to me, lest, if You be silent to me, I become like those going down to the pit [the grave].

²Hear the voice of my supplication as I cry to You for help, as I lift up my hands toward Your innermost sanctuary (the Holy of Holies).

³Drag me not away with the wicked, with the workers of iniquity, who speak peace with their neighbors, but malice and mischief are in their hearts.

⁴Repay them according to their work and according to the wickedness of their doings; repay them according to the work of their hands; render to them what they deserve.

⁵Because they regard not the works of the Lord nor the operations of His hands, He will break them down and not rebuild them.

⁶Blessed be the Lord, because He has heard the voice of my supplications.

⁷The Lord is my Strength and my [impenetrable] Shield; my heart trusts in, relies on, and confidently leans on Him, and I am helped; therefore my heart greatly rejoices, and with my song will I praise Him.

⁸The Lord is their [unyielding] Strength, and He is the Stronghold of salvation to [me] His anointed.

⁹Save Your people and bless Your heritage; nourish and shepherd them and carry them forever.

PSALM 29
A Psalm of David.

¹ASCRIBE TO the Lord, O sons of the mighty, ascribe to the Lord glory and strength.

²Give to the Lord the glory due to His name; worship the Lord in the beauty of holiness or in holy array.

³The voice of the Lord is upon the waters; the God of glory thunders; the Lord is upon many (great) waters.

⁴The voice of the Lord is powerful; the voice of the Lord is full of majesty.

⁵The voice of the Lord breaks the cedars; yes, the Lord breaks in pieces the cedars of Lebanon.

⁶He makes them also to skip like a calf; Lebanon and Sirion (Mount Hermon) like a young, wild ox.

⁷The voice of the Lord splits and flashes forth forked lightning.

⁸The voice of the Lord makes the wilderness tremble; the Lord shakes the Wilderness of Kadesh.

⁹The voice of the Lord makes the hinds bring forth their young, and His voice strips bare the forests, while in His temple everyone is saying, Glory!

¹⁰The Lord sat as King over the deluge; the Lord [still] sits as King [and] forever!

¹¹The Lord will give [unyielding and impenetrable] strength to His people; the Lord will bless His people with peace.

PSALM 30

A Psalm; a Song at the Dedication of the Temple.
[A Psalm] of David.

¹I WILL extol You, O Lord, for You have lifted me up and have not let my foes rejoice over me.

²O Lord my God, I cried to You and You have healed me.

³O Lord, You have brought my life up from Sheol (the place of the dead); You have kept me alive, that I should not go down to the pit (the grave).

⁴Sing to the Lord, O you saints of His, and give thanks at the remembrance of His holy name.

⁵For His anger is but for a moment, but His favor is for a lifetime or in His favor is life. Weeping may endure for a night, but joy comes in the morning.

⁶As for me, in my prosperity I said, I shall never be moved.

⁷By Your favor, O Lord, You have established me as a strong mountain; You hid Your face, and I was troubled.

⁸I cried to You, O Lord, and to the Lord I made supplication.

⁹What profit is there in my blood, when I go down to the pit (the grave)? Will the dust praise You? Will it declare Your truth and faithfulness to men?

¹⁰Hear, O Lord, have mercy and be gracious to me! O Lord, be my helper!

¹¹You have turned my mourning into dancing for me; You have put off my sackcloth and girded me with gladness,

¹²To the end that my tongue and my heart and everything glorious within me may sing praise to You and not be silent. O Lord my God, I will give thanks to You forever.

PSALM 31

To the Chief Musician. A Psalm of David.

¹IN YOU, O Lord, do I put my trust and seek refuge; let me never be put to shame or [have my hope in You] disappointed; deliver me in Your righteousness!

²Bow down Your ear to me, deliver me speedily! Be my Rock of refuge, a strong Fortress to save me!

³Yes, You are my Rock and my Fortress; therefore for Your name's sake lead me and guide me.

⁴Draw me out of the net that they have laid secretly for me, for You are my Strength and my Stronghold.

⁵Into Your hands I commit my spirit; You have redeemed me, O Lord, the God of truth and faithfulness.

⁶I abhor those who pay regard to vain idols; but I trust in, rely on, and confidently lean on the Lord.

⁷I will be glad and rejoice in Your mercy and steadfast love, because You have seen my affliction, You have taken note of my life's distresses,

⁸And You have not given me into the hand of the enemy; You have set my feet in a broad place.

⁹Have mercy and be gracious unto me, O Lord, for I am in trouble; with grief my eye is weakened, also my inner self and my body.

¹⁰For my life is spent with sorrow and my years with sighing; my strength has failed because of my iniquity, and even my bones have wasted away.

¹¹To all my enemies I have become a reproach, but especially to my neighbors, and a dread to my acquaintances, who flee from me on the street.

¹²I am forgotten like a dead man, and out of mind; like a broken vessel am I.

¹³For I have heard the slander of many; terror is on every side! While they schemed together against me, they plotted to take my life.

¹⁴But I trusted in, relied on, and was confident in You, O Lord; I said, You are my God.

¹⁵My times are in Your hands; deliver me from the hands of my foes and those who pursue me and persecute me.

¹⁶Let Your face shine on Your servant; save me for Your mercy's sake and in Your loving-kindness.

[17]Let me not be put to shame, O Lord, or disappointed, for I am calling upon You; let the wicked be put to shame, let them be silent in Sheol (place of the dead).

[18]Let the lying lips be silenced, which speak insolently against the [consistently] righteous with pride and contempt.

[19]Oh, how great is Your goodness, which You have laid up for those who fear, revere, and worship You, goodness which You have wrought for those who trust and take refuge in You before the sons of men!

[20]In the secret place of Your presence You hide them from the plots of men; You keep them secretly in Your pavilion from the strife of tongues.

[21]Blessed be the Lord! For He has shown me His marvelous loving favor when I was beset as in a besieged city.

[22]As for me, I said in my haste and alarm, I am cut off from before Your eyes. But You heard the voice of my supplications when I cried to You for aid.

[23]O love the Lord, all you His saints! The Lord preserves the faithful, and plentifully pays back him who deals haughtily.

[24]Be strong and let your heart take courage, all you who wait for and hope for and expect the Lord!

PSALM 32

A skillful song, or a didactic or reflective poem.

[1]BLESSED (HAPPY, fortunate, to be envied) is he who has forgiveness of his transgression continually exercised upon him, whose sin is covered.

[2]Blessed (happy, fortunate, to be envied) is the man to whom the Lord imputes no iniquity and in whose spirit there is no deceit.

[3]When I kept silence [before I confessed], my bones wasted away through my groaning all the day long.

[4]For day and night Your hand [of displeasure] was heavy upon me; my moisture was turned into the drought of summer. Selah [pause, and calmly think of that]!

[5]I acknowledged my sin to You, and my iniquity I did not hide. I said, I will confess my transgressions to the Lord [continually unfolding the past till all is told]--then You [instantly] forgave me the guilt and iniquity of my sin. Selah [pause, and calmly think of that]!

⁶For this [forgiveness] let everyone who is godly pray--pray to You in a time when You may be found; surely when the great waters [of trial] overflow, they shall not reach [the spirit in] him.

⁷You are a hiding place for me; You, Lord, preserve me from trouble, You surround me with songs and shouts of deliverance. Selah [pause, and calmly think of that]!

⁸I will instruct you and teach you in the way you should go; I will counsel you with My eye upon you.

⁹Be not like the horse or the mule, which lack understanding, which must have their mouths held firm with bit and bridle, or else they will not come with you.

¹⁰Many are the sorrows of the wicked, but he who trusts in, relies on, and confidently leans on the Lord shall be compassed about with mercy and with loving-kindness.

¹¹Be glad in the Lord and rejoice, you [uncompromisingly] righteous [you who are upright and in right standing with Him]; shout for joy, all you upright in heart!

PSALM 33

¹REJOICE IN the Lord, O you [uncompromisingly] righteous [you upright in right standing with God]; for praise is becoming and appropriate for those who are upright [in heart].

²Give thanks to the Lord with the lyre; sing praises to Him with the harp of ten strings.

³Sing to Him a new song; play skillfully [on the strings] with a loud and joyful sound.

⁴For the word of the Lord is right; and all His work is done in faithfulness.

⁵He loves righteousness and justice; the earth is full of the loving-kindness of the Lord.

⁶By the word of the Lord were the heavens made, and all their host by the breath of His mouth.

⁷He gathers the waters of the sea as in a bottle; He puts the deeps in storage places.

⁸Let all the earth fear the Lord [revere and worship Him]; let all the inhabitants of the world stand in awe of Him.

⁹For He spoke, and it was done; He commanded, and it stood fast.

[10]The Lord brings the counsel of the nations to nought; He makes the thoughts and plans of the peoples of no effect.

[11]The counsel of the Lord stands forever, the thoughts of His heart through all generations.

[12]Blessed (happy, fortunate, to be envied) is the nation whose God is the Lord, the people He has chosen as His heritage.

[13]The Lord looks from heaven, He beholds all the sons of men;

[14]From His dwelling place He looks [intently] upon all the inhabitants of the earth--

[15]He Who fashions the hearts of them all, Who considers all their doings.

[16]No king is saved by the great size and power of his army; a mighty man is not delivered by [his] much strength.

[17]A horse is devoid of value for victory; neither does he deliver any by his great power.

[18]Behold, the Lord's eye is upon those who fear Him [who revere and worship Him with awe], who wait for Him and hope in His mercy and loving-kindness,

[19]To deliver them from death and keep them alive in famine.

[20]Our inner selves wait [earnestly] for the Lord; He is our Help and our Shield.

[21]For in Him does our heart rejoice, because we have trusted (relied on and been confident) in His holy name.

[22]Let Your mercy and loving-kindness, O Lord, be upon us, in proportion to our waiting and hoping for You.

PSALM 34

[A Psalm] of David; when he pretended to be insane before
Abimelech, who drove him out, and he went away.

[1]I WILL bless the Lord at all times; His praise shall continually be in my mouth.

[2]My life makes its boast in the Lord; let the humble and afflicted hear and be glad.

[3]O magnify the Lord with me, and let us exalt His name together.

[4]I sought (inquired of) the Lord and required Him [of necessity and on the authority of His Word], and He heard me, and delivered me from all my fears.

[5]They looked to Him and were radiant; their faces shall never blush for shame or be confused.

[6]This poor man cried, and the Lord heard him, and saved him out of all his troubles.

[7]The Angel of the Lord encamps around those who fear Him [who revere and worship Him with awe] and each of them He delivers.

[8]O taste and see that the Lord [our God] is good! Blessed (happy, fortunate, to be envied) is the man who trusts and takes refuge in Him.

[9]O fear the Lord, you His saints [revere and worship Him]! For there is no want to those who truly revere and worship Him with godly fear.

[10]The young lions lack food and suffer hunger, but they who seek (inquire of and require) the Lord [by right of their need and on the authority of His Word], none of them shall lack any beneficial thing.

[11]Come, you children, listen to me; I will teach you to revere and worshipfully fear the Lord.

[12]What man is he who desires life and longs for many days, that he may see good?

[13]Keep your tongue from evil and your lips from speaking deceit.

[14]Depart from evil and do good; seek, inquire for, and crave peace and pursue (go after) it!

[15]The eyes of the Lord are toward the righteous and His ears are open to their cry.

[16]The face of the Lord is against those who do evil, to cut off the remembrance of them from the earth.

[17]When the righteous cry for help, the Lord hears, and delivers them out of all their distress and troubles.

[18]The Lord is close to those who are of a broken heart and saves such as are crushed with sorrow for sin and are humbly and thoroughly penitent.

[19]Many evils confront the [consistently] righteous, but the Lord delivers him out of them all.

[20]He keeps all his bones; not one of them is broken.

[21]Evil shall cause the death of the wicked; and they who hate the just and righteous shall be held guilty and shall be condemned.

[22]The Lord redeems the lives of His servants, and none of those who take refuge and trust in Him shall be condemned or held guilty.

PSALM 35

[A Psalm] of David.

¹CONTEND, O Lord, with those who contend with me; fight against those who fight against me!

²Take hold of shield and buckler, and stand up for my help!

³Draw out also the spear and javelin and close up the way of those who pursue and persecute me. Say to me, I am your deliverance!

⁴Let them be put to shame and dishonor who seek and require my life; let them be turned back and confounded who plan my hurt!

⁵Let them be as chaff before the wind, with the Angel of the Lord driving them on!

⁶Let their way be through dark and slippery places, with the Angel of the Lord pursuing and afflicting them.

⁷For without cause they hid for me their net; a pit of destruction without cause they dug for my life.

⁸Let destruction befall [my foe] unawares; let the net he hid for me catch him; let him fall into that very destruction.

⁹Then I shall be joyful in the Lord; I shall rejoice in His deliverance.

¹⁰All my bones shall say, Lord, who is like You, You Who deliver the poor and the afflicted from him who is too strong for him, yes, the poor and the needy from him who snatches away his goods?

¹¹Malicious and unrighteous witnesses rise up; they ask me of things that I know not.

¹²They reward me evil for good to my personal bereavement.

¹³But as for me, when they were sick, my clothing was sackcloth; I afflicted myself with fasting, and I prayed with head bowed on my breast.

¹⁴I behaved as if grieving for my friend or my brother; I bowed down in sorrow, as one who bewails his mother.

¹⁵But in my stumbling and limping they rejoiced and gathered together [against me]; the smiters (slanderers and revilers) gathered against me, and I knew them not; they ceased not to slander and revile me.

¹⁶Like profane mockers at feasts [making sport for the price of a cake] they gnashed at me with their teeth.

¹⁷Lord, how long will You look on [without action]? Rescue my life from their destructions, my dear and only life from the lions!

¹⁸I will give You thanks in the great assembly; I will praise You among a mighty throng.

¹⁹Let not those who are wrongfully my foes rejoice over me; neither let them wink with the eye who hate me without cause.

²⁰For they do not speak peace, but they devise deceitful matters against those who are quiet in the land.

²¹Yes, they open their mouths wide against me; they say, Aha! Aha! Our eyes have seen it!

²²You have seen this, O Lord; keep not silence! O Lord, be not far from me!

²³Arouse Yourself, awake to the justice due me, even to my cause, my God and my Lord!

²⁴Judge and vindicate me, O Lord my God, according to Your righteousness (Your rightness and justice); and let [my foes] not rejoice over me!

²⁵Let them not say in their hearts, Aha, that is what we wanted! Let them not say, We have swallowed him up and utterly destroyed him.

²⁶Let them be put to shame and confusion together who rejoice at my calamity! Let them be clothed with shame and dishonor who magnify and exalt themselves over me!

²⁷Let those who favor my righteous cause and have pleasure in my uprightness shout for joy and be glad and say continually, Let the Lord be magnified, Who takes pleasure in the prosperity of His servant.

²⁸And my tongue shall talk of Your righteousness, rightness, and justice, and of [my reasons for] Your praise all the day long.

PSALM 36

To the Chief Musician. [A Psalm] of David
the servant of the Lord.

¹TRANSGRESSION [like an oracle] speaks to the wicked deep in his heart. There is no fear or dread of God before his eyes.

²For he flatters and deceives himself in his own eyes that his iniquity will not be found out and be hated.

³The words of his mouth are wrong and deceitful; he has ceased to be wise and to do good.

⁴He plans wrongdoing on his bed; he sets himself in a way that is not good; he does not reject or despise evil.

⁵Your mercy and loving-kindness, O Lord, extend to the skies, and Your faithfulness to the clouds.

⁶Your righteousness is like the mountains of God, Your judgments are like the great deep. O Lord, You preserve man and beast.

⁷How precious is Your steadfast love, O God! The children of men take refuge and put their trust under the shadow of Your wings.

⁸They relish and feast on the abundance of Your house; and You cause them to drink of the stream of Your pleasures.

⁹For with You is the fountain of life; in Your light do we see light.

¹⁰O continue Your loving-kindness to those who know You, Your righteousness (salvation) to the upright in heart.

¹¹Let not the foot of pride overtake me, and let not the hand of the wicked drive me away.

¹²There the workers of iniquity fall and lie prostrate; they are thrust down and shall not be able to rise.

PSALM 37
[A Psalm] of David.

¹FRET NOT yourself because of evildoers, neither be envious against those who work unrighteousness (that which is not upright or in right standing with God).

²For they shall soon be cut down like the grass, and wither as the green herb.

³Trust (lean on, rely on, and be confident) in the Lord and do good; so shall you dwell in the land and feed surely on His faithfulness, and truly you shall be fed.

⁴Delight yourself also in the Lord, and He will give you the desires and secret petitions of your heart.

⁵Commit your way to the Lord [roll and repose each care of your load on Him]; trust (lean on, rely on, and be confident) also in Him and He will bring it to pass.

⁶And He will make your uprightness and right standing with God go forth as the light, and your justice and right as [the shining sun of] the noonday.

⁷Be still and rest in the Lord; wait for Him and patiently lean yourself upon Him; fret not yourself because of him who prospers in his way, because of the man who brings wicked devices to pass.

[8]Cease from anger and forsake wrath; fret not yourself--it tends only to evildoing.

[9]For evildoers shall be cut off, but those who wait and hope and look for the Lord [in the end] shall inherit the earth.

[10]For yet a little while, and the evildoers will be no more; though you look with care where they used to be, they will not be found.

[11]But the meek [in the end] shall inherit the earth and shall delight themselves in the abundance of peace.

[12]The wicked plot against the [uncompromisingly] righteous (the upright in right standing with God); they gnash at them with their teeth.

[13]The Lord laughs at [the wicked], for He sees that their own day [of defeat] is coming.

[14]The wicked draw the sword and bend their bows to cast down the poor and needy, to slay those who walk uprightly (blameless in conduct and in conversation).

[15]The swords [of the wicked] shall enter their own hearts, and their bows shall be broken.

[16]Better is the little that the [uncompromisingly] righteous have than the abundance [of possessions] of many who are wrong and wicked.

[17]For the arms of the wicked shall be broken, but the Lord upholds the [consistently] righteous.

[18]The Lord knows the days of the upright and blameless, and their heritage will abide forever.

[19]They shall not be put to shame in the time of evil; and in the days of famine they shall be satisfied.

[20]But the wicked shall perish, and the enemies of the Lord shall be as the fat of lambs [that is consumed in smoke] and as the glory of the pastures. They shall vanish; like smoke shall they consume away.

[21]The wicked borrow and pay not again [for they may be unable], but the [uncompromisingly] righteous deal kindly and give [for they are able].

[22]For such as are blessed of God shall [in the end] inherit the earth, but they that are cursed of Him shall be cut off.

[23]The steps of a [good] man are directed and established by the Lord when He delights in his way [and He busies Himself with his every step].

²⁴Though he falls, he shall not be utterly cast down, for the Lord grasps his hand in support and upholds him.

²⁵I have been young and now am old, yet have I not seen the [uncompromisingly] righteous forsaken or their seed begging bread.

²⁶All day long they are merciful and deal graciously; they lend, and their offspring are blessed.

²⁷Depart from evil and do good; and you will dwell forever [securely].

²⁸For the Lord delights in justice and forsakes not His saints; they are preserved forever, but the offspring of the wicked [in time] shall be cut off.

²⁹[Then] the [consistently] righteous shall inherit the land and dwell upon it forever.

³⁰The mouth of the [uncompromisingly] righteous utters wisdom, and his tongue speaks with justice.

³¹The law of his God is in his heart; none of his steps shall slide.

³²The wicked lie in wait for the [uncompromisingly] righteous and seek to put them to death.

³³The Lord will not leave them in their hands, or [suffer them to] condemn them when they are judged.

³⁴Wait for and expect the Lord and keep and heed His way, and He will exalt you to inherit the land; [in the end] when the wicked are cut off, you shall see it.

³⁵I have seen a wicked man in great power and spreading himself like a green tree in its native soil,

³⁶Yet he passed away, and behold, he was not; yes, I sought and inquired for him, but he could not be found.

³⁷Mark the blameless man and behold the upright, for there is a happy end for the man of peace.

³⁸As for transgressors, they shall be destroyed together; in the end the wicked shall be cut off.

³⁹But the salvation of the [consistently] righteous is of the Lord; He is their Refuge and secure Stronghold in the time of trouble.

⁴⁰And the Lord helps them and delivers them; He delivers them from the wicked and saves them, because they trust and take refuge in Him.

PSALM 38

A Psalm of David; to bring to remembrance
and make memorial.

[1]O LORD, rebuke me not in Your wrath, neither chasten me in Your hot displeasure.

[2]For Your arrows have sunk into me and stick fast, and Your hand has come down upon me and pressed me sorely.

[3]There is no soundness in my flesh because of Your indignation; neither is there any health or rest in my bones because of my sin.

[4]For my iniquities have gone over my head [like waves of a flood]; as a heavy burden they weigh too much for me.

[5]My wounds are loathsome and corrupt because of my foolishness.

[6]I am bent and bowed down greatly; I go about mourning all the day long.

[7]For my loins are filled with burning; and there is no soundness in my flesh.

[8]I am faint and sorely bruised [deadly cold and quite worn out]; I groan by reason of the disquiet and moaning of my heart.

[9]Lord, all my desire is before You; and my sighing is not hidden from You.

[10]My heart throbs, my strength fails me; as for the light of my eyes, it also is gone from me.

[11]My lovers and my friends stand aloof from my plague; my neighbors and near ones stand afar off.

[12]They also that seek and demand my life lay snares for me, and they that seek and require my hurt speak crafty and mischievous things; they meditate treachery and deceit all the day long.

[13]But I, like a deaf man, hear not; and I am like a dumb man who opens not his mouth.

[14]Yes, I have become like a man who hears not, in whose mouth are no arguments or replies.

[15]For in You, O Lord, do I hope; You will answer, O Lord my God.

[16]For I pray, Let them not rejoice over me, who when my foot slips boast against me.

[17]For I am ready to halt and fall; my pain and sorrow are continually before me.

[18]For I do confess my guilt and iniquity; I am filled with sorrow for my sin.

[19]But my enemies are vigorous and strong, and those who hate me wrongfully are multiplied.

[20]They also that render evil for good are adversaries to me, because I follow the thing that is good.

[21]Forsake me not, O Lord; O my God, be not far from me.

[22]Make haste to help me, O Lord, my Salvation.

PSALM 39

To the Chief Musician; for Jeduthun [founder of an official musical family]. A Psalm of David.

[1]I SAID, I will take heed and guard my ways, that I may sin not with my tongue; I will muzzle my mouth as with a bridle while the wicked are before me.

[2]I was dumb with silence, I held my peace without profit and had no comfort away from good, while my distress was renewed.

[3]My heart was hot within me. While I was musing, the fire burned; then I spoke with my tongue:

[4]Lord, make me to know my end and [to appreciate] the measure of my days--what it is; let me know and realize how frail I am [how transient is my stay here].

[5]Behold, You have made my days as [short as] handbreadths, and my lifetime is as nothing in Your sight. Truly every man at his best is merely a breath! Selah!

[6]Surely every man walks to and fro--like a shadow in a pantomime; surely for futility and emptiness he is in turmoil; each one heaps up riches, not knowing who will gather them.

[7]And now, Lord, what do I wait for and expect? My hope and expectation are in You.

[8]Deliver me from all my transgressions; make me not the scorn and reproach of the [self-confident] fool!

[9]I am dumb, I open not my mouth, for it is You Who has done it.

[10]Remove Your stroke away from me; I am consumed by the conflict and the blow of Your hand.

[11]When with rebukes You correct and chasten man for sin, You waste his beauty like a moth and what is dear to him consumes away; surely every man is a mere breath. Selah [pause, and think calmly of that]!

¹²Hear my prayer, O Lord, and give ear to my cry; hold not Your peace at my tears! For I am Your passing guest, a temporary resident, as all my fathers were.

¹³O look away from me and spare me, that I may recover cheerfulness and encouraging strength and know gladness before I go and am no more!

PSALM 40

To the Chief Musician. A Psalm of David.

¹I WAITED patiently and expectantly for the Lord; and He inclined to me and heard my cry.

²He drew me up out of a horrible pit [a pit of tumult and of destruction], out of the miry clay (froth and slime), and set my feet upon a rock, steadying my steps and establishing my goings.

³And He has put a new song in my mouth, a song of praise to our God. Many shall see and fear (worship) and put their trust and confident reliance in the Lord.

⁴Blessed (happy, fortunate, to be envied) is the man who makes the Lord his refuge and trust, and turns not to the proud or to followers of false gods.

⁵Many, O Lord my God, are the wonderful works which You have done, and Your thoughts toward us; no one can compare with You! If I should declare and speak of them, they are too many to be numbered.

⁶Sacrifice and offering You do not desire, nor have You delight in them; You have given me the capacity to hear and obey [Your law, a more valuable service than] burnt offerings and sin offerings [which] You do not require.

⁷Then said I, Behold, I come; in the volume of the book it is written of me;

⁸I delight to do Your will, O my God; yes, Your law is within my heart.

⁹I have proclaimed glad tidings of righteousness in the great assembly [tidings of uprightness with God]. Behold, I have not restrained my lips, as You know, O Lord.

¹⁰I have not concealed Your righteousness within my heart; I have proclaimed Your faithfulness and Your salvation. I have not hid away Your steadfast love and Your truth from the great assembly.

[11]Withhold not Your tender mercy from me, O Lord; let Your loving-kindness and Your truth continually preserve me!

[12]For innumerable evils have compassed me about; my iniquities have taken such hold on me that I am not able to look up. They are more than the hairs of my head, and my heart has failed me and forsaken me.

[13]Be pleased, O Lord, to deliver me; O Lord, make haste to help me!

[14]Let them be put to shame and confounded together who seek and require my life to destroy it; let them be driven backward and brought to dishonor who wish me evil and delight in my hurt!

[15]Let them be desolate by reason of their shame who say to me, Aha, aha!

[16]Let all those that seek and require You rejoice and be glad in You; let such as love Your salvation say continually, The Lord be magnified!

[17][As for me] I am poor and needy, yet the Lord takes thought and plans for me. You are my Help and my Deliverer. O my God, do not tarry!

PSALM 41

To the Chief Musician. A Psalm of David.

[1]BLESSED (HAPPY, fortunate, to be envied) is he who considers the weak and the poor; the Lord will deliver him in the time of evil and trouble.

[2]The Lord will protect him and keep him alive; he shall be called blessed in the land; and You will not deliver him to the will of his enemies.

[3]The Lord will sustain, refresh, and strengthen him on his bed of languishing; all his bed You [O Lord] will turn, change, and transform in his illness.

[4]I said, Lord, be merciful and gracious to me; heal my inner self, for I have sinned against You.

[5]My enemies speak evil of me, [saying], When will he die and his name perish?

[6]And when one comes to see me, he speaks falsehood and empty words, while his heart gathers mischievous gossip [against me]; when he goes away, he tells it abroad.

[7]All who hate me whisper together about me; against me do they devise my hurt [imagining the worst for me].

[8]An evil disease, say they, is poured out upon him and cleaves fast to him; and now that he is bedfast, he will not rise up again.

[9]Even my own familiar friend, in whom I trusted (relied on and was confident), who ate of my bread, has lifted up his heel against me.

[10]But You, O Lord, be merciful and gracious to me, and raise me up, that I may requite them.

[11]By this I know that You favor and delight in me, because my enemy does not triumph over me.

[12]And as for me, You have upheld me in my integrity and set me in Your presence forever.

[13]Blessed be the Lord, the God of Israel, from everlasting and to everlasting [from this age to the next, and forever]! Amen and Amen.

PSALM 42

To the Chief Musician. A skillful song, or a didactic or reflective poem, of the sons of Korah.

[1]AS THE hart pants and longs for the water brooks, so I pant and long for You, O God.

[2]My inner self thirsts for God, for the living God. When shall I come and behold the face of God?

[3]My tears have been my food day and night, while men say to me all day long, Where is your God?

[4]These things I [earnestly] remember and pour myself out within me: how I went slowly before the throng and led them in procession to the house of God [like a bandmaster before his band, timing the steps to the sound of music and the chant of song], with the voice of shouting and praise, a throng keeping festival.

[5]Why are you cast down, O my inner self? And why should you moan over me and be disquieted within me? Hope in God and wait expectantly for Him, for I shall yet praise Him, my Help and my God.

[6]O my God, my life is cast down upon me [and I find the burden more than I can bear]; therefore will I [earnestly] remember You from the land of the Jordan [River] and the [summits of Mount] Hermon, from the little mountain Mizar.

[7](Roaring) deep calls to [roaring] deep at the thunder of Your waterspouts; all Your breakers and Your rolling waves have gone over me.

[8]Yet the Lord will command His loving-kindness in the daytime, and in the night His song shall be with me, a prayer to the God of my life.

[9]I will say to God my Rock, Why have You forgotten me? Why go I mourning because of the oppression of the enemy?

[10]As with a sword [crushing] in my bones, my enemies taunt and reproach me, while they say continually to me, Where is your God?

[11]Why are you cast down, O my inner self? And why should you moan over me and be disquieted within me? Hope in God and wait expectantly for Him, for I shall yet praise Him, Who is the help of my countenance, and my God.

PSALM 43

[1]JUDGE and vindicate me, O God; plead and defend my cause against an ungodly nation. O deliver me from the deceitful and unjust man!

[2]For You are the God of my strength [in Whom I take refuge]; why have You cast me off? Why go I mourning because of the oppression of the enemy?

[3]O send out Your light and Your truth, let them lead me; let them bring me to Your holy hill and to Your dwelling.

[4]Then will I go to the altar of God, to God, my exceeding joy; yes, with the lyre will I praise You, O God, my God!

[5]Why are you cast down, O my inner self? And why should you moan over me and be disquieted within me? Hope in God and wait expectantly for Him, for I shall yet praise Him, Who is the help of my [sad] countenance, and my God.

PSALM 44

To the Chief Musician. [A Psalm] of the sons of Korah.
A skillful song, or a didactic or reflective poem.

[1]WE HAVE heard with our ears, O God; our fathers have told us [what] work You did in their days, in the days of old.

²You drove out the nations with Your hand and it was Your power that gave [Israel] a home by rooting out the [heathen] peoples, but [Israel] You spread out.

³For they got not the land [of Canaan] in possession by their own sword, neither did their own arm save them; but Your right hand and Your arm and the light of Your countenance [did it], because You were favorable toward and did delight in them.

⁴You are my King, O God; command victories and deliverance for Jacob (Israel).

⁵Through You shall we push down our enemies; through Your name shall we tread them under who rise up against us.

⁶For I will not trust in and lean on my bow, neither shall my sword save me.

⁷But You have saved us from our foes and have put them to shame who hate us.

⁸In God we have made our boast all the day long, and we will give thanks to Your name forever. Selah [pause, and calmly think of that]!

⁹But now You have cast us off and brought us to dishonor, and You go not out with our armies.

¹⁰You make us to turn back from the enemy, and they who hate us take spoil for themselves.

¹¹You have made us like sheep intended for mutton and have scattered us in exile among the nations.

¹²You sell Your people for nothing, and have not increased Your wealth by their price.

¹³You have made us the taunt of our neighbors, a scoffing and a derision to those who are around us.

¹⁴You make us a byword among the nations, a shaking of the heads among the people.

¹⁵My dishonor is before me all day long, and shame has covered my face

¹⁶At the words of the taunter and reviler, by reason of the enemy and the revengeful.

¹⁷All this is come upon us, yet have we not forgotten You, neither have we been false to Your covenant [which You made with our fathers].

¹⁸Our hearts are not turned back, neither have our steps declined from Your path,

[19]Though You have distressingly broken us in the place of jackals and covered us with deep darkness, even with the shadow of death.

[20]If we had forgotten the name of our God or stretched out our hands to a strange god,

[21]Would not God discover this? For He knows the secrets of the heart.

[22]No, but for Your sake we are killed all the day long; we are accounted as sheep for the slaughter.

[23]Awake! Why do You sleep, O Lord? Arouse Yourself, cast us not off forever!

[24]Why do You hide Your face and forget our affliction and our oppression?

[25]For our lives are bowed down to the dust; our bodies cleave to the ground.

[26]Rise up! Come to our help, and deliver us for Your mercy's sake and because of Your steadfast love!

PSALM 45

To the Chief Musician; [set to the tune of] "Lilies" [probably a popular air. A Psalm] of the sons of Korah. A skillful song, or a didactic or reflective poem.
A song of love.

[1]MY HEART overflows with a goodly theme; I address my psalm to a King. My tongue is like the pen of a ready writer.

[2]You are fairer than the children of men; graciousness is poured upon Your lips; therefore God has blessed You forever.

[3]Gird Your sword upon Your thigh, O mighty One, in Your glory and Your majesty!

[4]And in Your majesty ride on triumphantly for the cause of truth, humility, and righteousness (uprightness and right standing with God); and let Your right hand guide You to tremendous things.

[5]Your arrows are sharp; the peoples fall under You; Your darts pierce the hearts of the King's enemies.

[6]Your throne, O God, is forever and ever; the scepter of righteousness is the scepter of Your kingdom.

[7]You love righteousness, uprightness, and right standing with God and hate wickedness; therefore God, Your God, has anointed You with the oil of gladness above Your fellows.

⁸Your garments are all fragrant with myrrh, aloes, and cassia; stringed instruments make You glad.

⁹Kings' daughters are among Your honorable women; at Your right hand stands the queen in gold of Ophir.

¹⁰Hear, O daughter, consider, submit, and consent to my instruction: forget also your own people and your father's house;

¹¹So will the King desire your beauty; because He is your Lord, be submissive and reverence and honor Him.

¹²And, O daughter of Tyre, the richest of the people shall entreat your favor with a gift.

¹³The King's daughter in the inner part [of the palace] is all glorious; her clothing is inwrought with gold.

¹⁴She shall be brought to the King in raiment of needlework; with the virgins, her companions that follow her, she shall be brought to You.

¹⁵With gladness and rejoicing will they be brought; they will enter into the King's palace.

¹⁶Instead of Your fathers shall be Your sons, whom You will make princes in all the land.

¹⁷I will make Your name to be remembered in all generations; therefore shall the people praise and give You thanks forever and ever.

PSALM 46
To the Chief Musician. [A Psalm] of the sons of Korah,
set to treble voices. A song.

¹GOD IS our Refuge and Strength [mighty and impenetrable to temptation], a very present and well-proved help in trouble.

²Therefore we will not fear, though the earth should change and though the mountains be shaken into the midst of the seas,

³Though its waters roar and foam, though the mountains tremble at its swelling and tumult. Selah [pause, and calmly think of that]!

⁴There is a river whose streams shall make glad the city of God, the holy place of the tabernacles of the Most High.

⁵God is in the midst of her, she shall not be moved; God will help her right early [at the dawn of the morning].

⁶The nations raged, the kingdoms tottered and were moved; He uttered His voice, the earth melted.

[7]The Lord of hosts is with us; the God of Jacob is our Refuge (our Fortress and High Tower). Selah [pause, and calmly think of that]!

[8]Come, behold the works of the Lord, Who has wrought desolations and wonders in the earth.

[9]He makes wars to cease to the end of the earth; He breaks the bow into pieces and snaps the spear in two; He burns the chariots in the fire.

[10]Let be and be still, and know (recognize and understand) that I am God. I will be exalted among the nations! I will be exalted in the earth!

[11]The Lord of hosts is with us; the God of Jacob is our Refuge (our High Tower and Stronghold). Selah [pause, and calmly think of that]!

PSALM 47

To the Chief Musician. A Psalm of the sons of Korah.

[1]O CLAP your hands, all you peoples! Shout to God with the voice of triumph and songs of joy!

[2]For the Lord Most High excites terror, awe, and dread; He is a great King over all the earth.

[3]He subdued peoples under us, and nations under our feet.

[4]He chose our inheritance for us, the glory and pride of Jacob, whom He loves. Selah [pause, and calmly think of that]!

[5]God has ascended amid shouting, the Lord with the sound of a trumpet.

[6]Sing praises to God, sing praises! Sing praises to our King, sing praises!

[7]For God is the King of all the earth; sing praises in a skillful psalm and with understanding.

[8]God reigns over the nations; God sits upon His holy throne.

[9]The princes and nobles of the peoples are gathered together, a [united] people for the God of Abraham, for the shields of the earth belong to God; He is highly exalted.

PSALM 48

A song; a Psalm of the sons of Korah.

¹GREAT IS the Lord, and highly to be praised in the city of our God! His holy mountain,

²Fair and beautiful in elevation, is the joy of all the earth--Mount Zion [the City of David], to the northern side [Mount Moriah and the temple], the [whole] city of the Great King!

³God has made Himself known in her palaces as a Refuge (a High Tower and a Stronghold).

⁴For, behold, the kings assembled, they came onward and they passed away together.

⁵They looked, they were amazed; they were stricken with terror and took to flight [affrighted and dismayed].

⁶Trembling took hold of them there, and pain as of a woman in childbirth.

⁷With the east wind You shattered the ships of Tarshish.

⁸As we have heard, so have we seen in the city of the Lord of hosts, in the city of our God: God will establish it forever. Selah [pause, and calmly think of that]!

⁹We have thought of Your steadfast love, O God, in the midst of Your temple.

¹⁰As is Your name, O God, so is Your praise to the ends of the earth; Your right hand is full of righteousness (rightness and justice).

¹¹Let Mount Zion be glad! Let the daughters of Judah rejoice because of Your [righteous] judgments!

¹²Walk about Zion, and go round about her, number her towers (her lofty and noble deeds of past days),

¹³Consider well her ramparts, go through her palaces and citadels, that you may tell the next generation [and cease recalling disappointments].

¹⁴For this God is our God forever and ever; He will be our guide [even] until death.

PSALM 49

To the Chief Musician. A Psalm of the sons of Korah.

¹HEAR THIS, all you peoples; give ear, all you inhabitants of the world,

²Both low and high, rich and poor together:

³My mouth shall speak wisdom; and the meditation of my heart shall be understanding.

⁴I will submit and consent to a parable or proverb; to the music of a lyre I will unfold my riddle (my problem).

⁵Why should I fear in the days of evil, when the iniquity of those who would supplant me surrounds me on every side,

⁶Even of those who trust in and lean on their wealth and boast of the abundance of their riches?

⁷None of them can by any means redeem [either himself or] his brother, nor give to God a ransom for him--

⁸For the ransom of a life is too costly, and [the price one can pay] can never suffice--

⁹So that he should live on forever and never see the pit (the grave) and corruption.

¹⁰For he sees that even wise men die; the [self-confident] fool and the stupid alike perish and leave their wealth to others.

¹¹Their inward thought is that their houses will continue forever, and their dwelling places to all generations; they call their lands their own [apart from God] and after their own names.

¹²But man, with all his honor and pomp, does not remain; he is like the beasts that perish.

¹³This is the fate of those who are foolishly confident, yet after them men approve their sayings. Selah [pause, and calmly think of that]!

¹⁴Like sheep they are appointed for Sheol (the place of the dead); death shall be their shepherd. And the upright shall have dominion over them in the morning; and their form and beauty shall be consumed, for Sheol shall be their dwelling.

¹⁵But God will redeem me from the power of Sheol (the place of the dead); for He will receive me. Selah [pause, and calmly think of that]!

¹⁶Be not afraid when [an ungodly] one is made rich, when the wealth and glory of his house are increased;

¹⁷For when he dies he will carry nothing away; his glory will not descend after him.

[18]Though while he lives he counts himself happy and prosperous, and though a man gets praise when he does well [for himself],

[19]He will go to the generation of his fathers, who will nevermore see the light.

[20]A man who is held in honor and understands not is like the beasts that perish.

PSALM 50

A Psalm of Asaph

[1]THE MIGHTY One, God, the Lord, speaks and calls the earth from the rising of the sun to its setting.

[2]Out of Zion, the perfection of beauty, God shines forth.

[3]Our God comes and does not keep silence; a fire devours before Him, and round about Him a mighty tempest rages.

[4]He calls to the heavens above and to the earth, that He may judge His people:

[5]Gather together to Me My saints [those who have found grace in My sight], those who have made a covenant with Me by sacrifice.

[6]And the heavens declare His righteousness (rightness and justice), for God, He is judge. Selah [pause, and calmly think of that]!

[7]Hear, O My people, and I will speak; O Israel, I will testify to you and against you: I am God, your God.

[8]I do not reprove you for your sacrifices; your burnt offerings are continually before Me.

[9]I will accept no bull from your house nor he-goat out of your folds.

[10]For every beast of the forest is Mine, and the cattle upon a thousand hills or upon the mountains where thousands are.

[11]I know and am acquainted with all the birds of the mountains, and the wild animals of the field are Mine and are with Me, in My mind.

[12]If I were hungry, I would not tell you, for the world and its fullness are Mine.

[13]Shall I eat the flesh of bulls or drink the blood of goats?

[14]Offer to God the sacrifice of thanksgiving, and pay your vows to the Most High,

[15]And call on Me in the day of trouble; I will deliver you, and you shall honor and glorify Me.

[16]But to the wicked, God says: What right have you to recite My statutes or take My covenant or pledge on your lips,

[17]Seeing that you hate instruction and correction and cast My words behind you [discarding them]?

[18]When you see a thief, you associate with him, and you have taken part with adulterers.

[19]You give your mouth to evil, and your tongue frames deceit.

[20]You sit and speak against your brother; you slander your own mother's son.

[21]These things you have done and I kept silent; you thought I was once entirely like you. But I will reprove you and put [the charge] in order before your eyes.

[22]Now consider this, you who forget God, lest I tear you in pieces, and there be none to deliver.

[23]He who brings an offering of praise and thanksgiving honors and glorifies Me; and he who orders his way aright [who prepares the way that I may show him], to him I will demonstrate the salvation of God.

PSALM 51

To the Chief Musician. A Psalm of David; when Nathan the prophet came to him after he had sinned with Bathsheba.

[1]HAVE MERCY upon me, O God, according to Your steadfast love; according to the multitude of Your tender mercy and loving-kindness blot out my transgressions.

[2]Wash me thoroughly [and repeatedly] from my iniquity and guilt and cleanse me and make me wholly pure from my sin!

[3]For I am conscious of my transgressions and I acknowledge them; my sin is ever before me.

[4]Against You, You only, have I sinned and done that which is evil in Your sight, so that You are justified in Your sentence and faultless in Your judgment.

[5]Behold, I was brought forth in [a state of] iniquity; my mother was sinful who conceived me [and I too am sinful].

[6]Behold, You desire truth in the inner being; make me therefore to know wisdom in my inmost heart.

[7]Purify me with hyssop, and I shall be clean [ceremonially]; wash

me, and I shall be whiter than snow.

⁸Make me to hear joy and gladness and be satisfied; let the bones which You have broken rejoice.

⁹Hide Your face from my sins and blot out all my guilt and iniquities.

¹⁰Create in me a clean heart, O God, and renew a right, persevering, and steadfast spirit within me.

¹¹Cast me not away from Your presence and take not Your Holy Spirit from me.

¹²Restore to me the joy of Your salvation and uphold me with a willing spirit.

¹³Then will I teach transgressors Your ways, and sinners shall be converted and return to You.

¹⁴Deliver me from bloodguiltiness and death, O God, the God of my salvation, and my tongue shall sing aloud of Your righteousness (Your rightness and Your justice).

¹⁵O Lord, open my lips, and my mouth shall show forth Your praise.

¹⁶For You delight not in sacrifice, or else would I give it; You find no pleasure in burnt offering.

¹⁷My sacrifice [the sacrifice acceptable] to God is a broken spirit; a broken and a contrite heart [broken down with sorrow for sin and humbly and thoroughly penitent], such, O God, You will not despise.

¹⁸Do good in Your good pleasure to Zion; rebuild the walls of Jerusalem.

¹⁹Then will You delight in the sacrifices of righteousness, justice, and right, with burnt offering and whole burnt offering; then bullocks will be offered upon Your altar.

PSALM 52

*To the Chief Musician. A skillful song, or a didactic
or reflective poem. [A Psalm] of David, when Doeg
the Edomite came and told Saul, David has come
to the house of Ahimelech.*

¹WHY BOAST you of mischief done against the loving-kindness of God [and the godly], O mighty [sinful] man, day after day?

²Your tongue devises wickedness; it is like a sharp razor, working deceitfully.

³You love evil more than good, and lying rather than to speak righteousness, justice, and right. Selah [pause, and calmly think of that]!

⁴You love all destroying and devouring words, O deceitful tongue.

⁵God will likewise break you down and destroy you forever; He will lay hold of you and pluck you out of your tent and uproot you from the land of the living. Selah [pause, and calmly think of that]!

⁶The [uncompromisingly] righteous also shall see [it] and be in reverent fear and awe, but about you they will [scoffingly] laugh, saying,

⁷See, this is the man who made not God his strength (his stronghold and high tower) but trusted in and confidently relied on the abundance of his riches, seeking refuge and security for himself through his wickedness.

⁸But I am like a green olive tree in the house of God; I trust in and confidently rely on the loving-kindness and the mercy of God forever and ever.

⁹I will thank You and confide in You forever, because You have done it [delivered me and kept me safe]. I will wait on, hope in and expect in Your name, for it is good, in the presence of Your saints (Your kind and pious ones).

PSALM 53

To the Chief Musician; in a mournful strain. A skillful song, or didactic or reflective poem of David.

¹THE [empty-headed] fool has said in his heart, There is no God. Corrupt and evil are they, and doing abominable iniquity; there is none who does good.

²God looked down from heaven upon the children of men to see if there were any who understood, who sought (inquired after and desperately required) God.

³Every one of them has gone back [backslidden and fallen away]; they have altogether become filthy and corrupt; there is none who does good, no, not one.

⁴Have those who work evil no knowledge (no understanding)? They eat up My people as they eat bread; they do not call upon God.

⁵There they are, in terror and dread, where there was [and had been] no terror and dread! For God has scattered the bones of him who encamps against you; you have put them to shame, because God has rejected them.

⁶Oh, that the salvation and deliverance of Israel would come out of Zion! When God restores the fortunes of His people, then will Jacob rejoice and Israel be glad.

PSALM 54

To the Chief Musician; with stringed instruments. A skillful song, or a didactic or reflective poem, of David, when the Ziphites went and told Saul, David is hiding among us.

¹SAVE ME, O God, by Your name; judge and vindicate me by Your mighty strength and power.

²Hear my pleading and my prayer, O God; give ear to the words of my mouth.

³For strangers and insolent men are rising up against me, and violent men and ruthless ones seek and demand my life; they do not set God before them. Selah [pause, and calmly think of that]!

⁴Behold, God is my helper and ally; the Lord is my upholder and is with them who uphold my life.

⁵He will pay back evil to my enemies; in Your faithfulness [Lord] put an end to them.

⁶With a freewill offering I will sacrifice to You; I will give thanks and praise Your name, O Lord, for it is good.

⁷For He has delivered me out of every trouble, and my eye has looked [in triumph] on my enemies.

PSALM 55

To the Chief Musician; with stringed instruments. A skillful song, or a didactic or reflective poem, of David.

¹LISTEN TO my prayer, O God, and hide not Yourself from my supplication!

²Attend to me and answer me; I am restless and distraught in my complaint and must moan

³[And I am distracted] at the noise of the enemy, because of the oppression and threats of the wicked; for they would cast trouble upon me, and in wrath they persecute me.

⁴My heart is grievously pained within me, and the terrors of death have fallen upon me.

⁵Fear and trembling have come upon me; horror and fright have overwhelmed me.

⁶And I say, Oh, that I had wings like a dove! I would fly away and be at rest.

⁷Yes, I would wander far away, I would lodge in the wilderness. Selah [pause, and calmly think of that]!

⁸I would hasten to escape and to find a shelter from the stormy wind and tempest.

⁹Destroy [their schemes], O Lord, confuse their tongues, for I have seen violence and strife in the city.

¹⁰Day and night they go about on its walls; iniquity and mischief are in its midst.

¹¹Violence and ruin are within it; fraud and guile do not depart from its streets and marketplaces.

¹²For it is not an enemy who reproaches and taunts me--then I might bear it; nor is it one who has hated me who insolently vaunts himself against me--then I might hide from him.

¹³But it was you, a man my equal, my companion and my familiar friend.

¹⁴We had sweet fellowship together and used to walk to the house of God in company.

¹⁵Let desolations and death come suddenly upon them; let them go down alive to Sheol (the place of the dead), for evils are in their habitations, in their hearts, and their inmost part.

¹⁶As for me, I will call upon God, and the Lord will save me.

¹⁷Evening and morning and at noon will I utter my complaint and moan and sigh, and He will hear my voice.

¹⁸He has redeemed my life in peace from the battle that was against me [so that none came near me], for they were many who strove with me.

¹⁹God will hear and humble them, even He Who abides of old--Selah [pause, and calmly think of that]!--because in them there has been no change [of heart], and they do not fear, revere, and worship God.

²⁰[My companion] has put forth his hands against those who were at peace with him; he has broken and profaned his agreement [of friendship and loyalty].

²¹The words of his mouth were smoother than cream or butter, but war was in his heart; his words were softer than oil, yet they were drawn swords.

²²Cast your burden on the Lord [releasing the weight of it] and He will sustain you; He will never allow the [consistently] righteous to be moved (made to slip, fall, or fail).

²³But You, O God, will bring down the wicked into the pit of destruction; men of blood and treachery shall not live out half their days. But I will trust in, lean on, and confidently rely on You.

PSALM 56

To the Chief Musician; [set to the tune of] "Silent Dove Among Those Far Away." Of David. A record of memorable thoughts when the Philistines seized him in Gath.

¹BE MERCIFUL and gracious to me, O God, for man would trample me or devour me; all the day long the adversary oppresses me.

²They that lie in wait for me would swallow me up or trample me all day long, for they are many who fight against me, O Most High!

³What time I am afraid, I will have confidence in and put my trust and reliance in You.

⁴By [the help of] God I will praise His word; on God I lean, rely, and confidently put my trust; I will not fear. What can man, who is flesh, do to me?

⁵All day long they twist my words and trouble my affairs; all their thoughts are against me for evil and my hurt.

⁶They gather themselves together, they hide themselves, they watch my steps, even as they have [expectantly] waited for my life.

⁷They think to escape with iniquity, and shall they? In Your indignation bring down the peoples, O God.

⁸You number and record my wanderings; put my tears into Your bottle--are they not in Your book?

⁹Then shall my enemies turn back in the day that I cry out; this I know, for God is for me.

¹⁰In God, Whose word I praise, in the Lord, Whose word I praise,

¹¹In God have I put my trust and confident reliance; I will not be afraid. What can man do to me?

¹²Your vows are upon me, O God; I will render praise to You and give You thank offerings.

¹³For You have delivered my life from death, yes, and my feet from falling, that I may walk before God in the light of life and of the living.

PSALM 57

To the Chief Musician; [set to the tune of] "Do Not Destroy." A record of memorable thoughts of David when he fled from Saul in the cave.

¹BE MERCIFUL and gracious to me, O God, be merciful and gracious to me, for my soul takes refuge and finds shelter and confidence in You; yes, in the shadow of Your wings will I take refuge and be confident until calamities and destructive storms are passed.

²I will cry to God Most High, Who performs on my behalf and rewards me [Who brings to pass His purposes for me and surely completes them]!

³He will send from heaven and save me from the slanders and reproaches of him who would trample me down or swallow me up, and He will put him to shame. Selah [pause, and calmly think of that]! God will send forth His mercy and loving-kindness and His truth and faithfulness.

⁴My life is among lions; I must lie among those who are aflame--the sons of men whose teeth are spears and arrows, their tongues sharp swords.

⁵Be exalted, O God, above the heavens! Let Your glory be over all the earth!

⁶They set a net for my steps; my very life was bowed down. They dug a pit in my way; into the midst of it they themselves have fallen. Selah [pause, and calmly think of that]!

⁷My heart is fixed, O God, my heart is steadfast and confident! I will sing and make melody.

⁸Awake, my glory (my inner self); awake, harp and lyre! I will awake right early [I will awaken the dawn]!

⁹I will praise and give thanks to You, O Lord, among the peoples; I will sing praises to You among the nations.

¹⁰For Your mercy and loving-kindness are great, reaching to the heavens, and Your truth and faithfulness to the clouds.

¹¹Be exalted, O God, above the heavens; let Your glory be over all the earth.

PSALM 58

To the Chief Musician; [set to the tune of] "Do Not Destroy." A record of memorable thoughts of David.

¹DO YOU indeed in silence speak righteousness, O you mighty ones? [Or is the righteousness, rightness, and justice you should speak quite dumb?] Do you judge fairly and uprightly, O you sons of men?

²No, in your heart you devise wickedness; you deal out in the land the violence of your hands.

³The ungodly are perverse and estranged from the womb; they go astray as soon as they are born, speaking lies.

⁴Their poison is like the venom of a serpent; they are like the deaf adder or asp that stops its ear,

⁵Which listens not to the voice of charmers or of the enchanter never casting spells so cunningly.

⁶Break their teeth, O God, in their mouths; break out the fangs of the young lions, O Lord.

⁷Let them melt away as water which runs on apace; when he aims his arrows, let them be as if they were headless or split apart.

⁸Let them be as a snail dissolving slime as it passes on or as a festering sore which wastes away, like [the child to which] a woman gives untimely birth that has not seen the sun.

⁹Before your pots can feel the thorns [that are placed under them for fuel], He will take them away as with a whirlwind, the green and the burning ones alike.

¹⁰The [unyieldingly] righteous shall rejoice when he sees the vengeance; he will bathe his feet in the blood of the wicked.

¹¹Men will say, Surely there is a reward for the righteous; surely there is a God Who judges on the earth.

PSALM 59

*To the Chief Musician; [set to the tune of] "Do Not Destroy." Of
David, a record of memorable thoughts when Saul
sent men to watch his house in order to kill him.*

¹DELIVER ME from my enemies, O my God; defend and protect me from those who rise up against me.

²Deliver me from and lift me above those who work evil and save me from bloodthirsty men.

³For, behold, they lie in wait for my life; fierce and mighty men are banding together against me, not for my transgression nor for any sin of mine, O Lord.

⁴They run and prepare themselves, though there is no fault in me; rouse Yourself [O Lord] to meet and help me, and see!

⁵You, O Lord God of hosts, the God of Israel, arise to visit all the nations; spare none and be not merciful to any who treacherously plot evil. Selah [pause, and calmly think of that]!

⁶They return at evening, they howl and snarl like dogs, and go [prowling] about the city.

⁷Behold, they belch out [insults] with their mouths; swords [of sarcasm, ridicule, slander, and lies] are in their lips, for who, they think, hears us?

⁸But You, O Lord, will laugh at them [in scorn]; You will hold all the nations in derision.

⁹O my Strength, I will watch and give heed to You and sing praises; for God is my Defense my Protector.

¹⁰My God in His mercy and steadfast love will meet me; God will let me look [triumphantly] on my enemies (those who lie in wait for me).

¹¹Slay them not, lest my people forget; scatter them by Your power and make them wander to and fro, and bring them down, O Lord our Shield!

¹²For the sin of their mouths and the words of their lips, let them even be trapped and taken in their pride, and for the cursing and lying which they utter.

¹³Consume them in wrath, consume them so that they shall be no more; and let them know unto the ends of the earth that God rules over Jacob (Israel). Selah [pause, and calmly think of that]!

¹⁴And at evening let them return; let them howl and snarl like dogs, and go prowling about the city.

[15]Let them wander up and down for food and tarry all night if they are not satisfied (not getting their fill).

[16]But I will sing of Your mighty strength and power; yes, I will sing aloud of Your mercy and loving-kindness in the morning; for You have been to me a defense (a fortress and a high tower) and a refuge in the day of my distress.

[17]Unto You, O my Strength, I will sing praises; for God is my Defense, my Fortress, and High Tower, the God Who shows me mercy and steadfast love.

PSALM 60

To the Chief Musician; [set to the tune of] "The Lily of the Testimony."

A poem of David intended to record memorable thoughts and to teach; when he had striven with the Arameans of Mesopotamia and the Arameans of Zobah, and when Joab returned and smote twelve thousand Edomites in the Valley of Salt.

[1]O GOD, You have rejected us and cast us off, broken down [our defenses], and scattered us; You have been angry--O restore us and turn Yourself to us again!

[2]You have made the land to quake and tremble, You have rent it [open]; repair its breaches, for it shakes and totters.

[3]You have made Your people suffer hard things; You have given us to drink wine that makes us reel and be dazed.

[4][But now] You have set up a banner for those who fear and worshipfully revere You [to which they may flee from the bow], a standard displayed because of the truth. Selah [pause, and calmly think of that]!

[5]That Your beloved ones may be delivered, save with Your right hand and answer us [or me].

[6]God has spoken in His holiness [in His promises]: I will rejoice, I will divide and portion out [the land] Shechem and the Valley of Succoth [west to east].

[7]Gilead is Mine, and Manasseh is Mine; Ephraim also is My helmet (the defense of My head); Judah is My scepter and My lawgiver.

[8]Moab is My washpot [reduced to vilest servitude]; upon Edom I cast My shoe in triumph; over Philistia I raise the shout of victory.

⁹Who will bring me [David] into the strong city [of Petra]? Who will lead me into Edom?

¹⁰Have You not rejected us, O God? And will You not go forth, O God, with our armies?

¹¹O give us help against the adversary, for vain (ineffectual and to no purpose) is the help or salvation of man.

¹²Through God we shall do valiantly, for He it is Who shall tread down our adversaries.

PSALM 61

To the Chief Musician; on stringed instruments.
[A Psalm] of David.

¹HEAR MY cry, O God; listen to my prayer.

²From the end of the earth will I cry to You, when my heart is overwhelmed and fainting; lead me to the rock that is higher than I [yes, a rock that is too high for me].

³For You have been a shelter and a refuge for me, a strong tower against the adversary.

⁴I will dwell in Your tabernacle forever; let me find refuge and trust in the shelter of Your wings. Selah [pause, and calmly think of that]!

⁵For You, O God, have heard my vows; You have given me the heritage of those who fear, revere, and honor Your name.

⁶May You prolong the [true] King's life [adding days upon days], and may His years be to the last generation [of this world and the generations of the world to come].

⁷May He sit enthroned forever before [the face of] God; O ordain that loving-kindness and faithfulness may watch over Him!

⁸So will I sing praise to Your name forever, paying my vows day by day.

PSALM 62

To the Chief Musician; according to Jeduthun [Ethan, the noted musician, founder of an official musical family]. A Psalm of David.

¹FOR GOD alone my soul waits in silence; from Him comes my salvation.

²He only is my Rock and my Salvation, my Defense and my Fortress, I shall not be greatly moved.

³How long will you set upon a man that you may slay him, all of you, like a leaning wall, like a tottering fence?

⁴They only consult to cast him down from his height [to dishonor him]; they delight in lies. They bless with their mouths, but they curse inwardly. Selah [pause, and calmly think of that]!

⁵My soul, wait only upon God and silently submit to Him; for my hope and expectation are from Him.

⁶He only is my Rock and my Salvation; He is my Defense and my Fortress, I shall not be moved.

⁷With God rests my salvation and my glory; He is my Rock of unyielding strength and impenetrable hardness, and my refuge is in God!

⁸Trust in, lean on, rely on, and have confidence in Him at all times, you people; pour out your hearts before Him. God is a refuge for us (a fortress and a high tower). Selah [pause, and calmly think of that]!

⁹Men of low degree [in the social scale] are emptiness (futility, a breath) and men of high degree [in the same scale] are a lie and a delusion. In the balances they go up; they are together lighter than a breath.

¹⁰Trust not in and rely confidently not on extortion and oppression, and do not vainly hope in robbery; if riches increase, set not your heart on them.

¹¹God has spoken once, twice have I heard this: that power belongs to God.

¹²Also to You, O Lord, belong mercy and loving-kindness, for You render to every man according to his work.

PSALM 63

A Psalm of David; when he was in the Wilderness of Judah.

¹O GOD, You are my God, earnestly will I seek You; my inner self thirsts for You, my flesh longs and is faint for You, in a dry and weary land where no water is.

²So I have looked upon You in the sanctuary to see Your power and Your glory.

³Because Your loving-kindness is better than life, my lips shall praise You.

⁴So will I bless You while I live; I will lift up my hands in Your name.

⁵My whole being shall be satisfied as with marrow and fatness; and my mouth shall praise You with joyful lips

⁶When I remember You upon my bed and meditate on You in the night watches.

⁷For You have been my help, and in the shadow of Your wings will I rejoice.

⁸My whole being follows hard after You and clings closely to You; Your right hand upholds me.

⁹But those who seek and demand my life to ruin and destroy it shall [themselves be destroyed and] go into the lower parts of the earth [into the underworld of the dead].

¹⁰They shall be given over to the power of the sword; they shall be a prey for foxes and jackals.

¹¹But the king shall rejoice in God; everyone who swears by Him [that is, who binds himself by God's authority, acknowledging His supremacy, and devoting himself to His glory and service alone] shall glory, for the mouths of those who speak lies shall be stopped.

PSALM 64

To the Chief Musician. A Psalm of David.

¹HEAR MY voice, O God, in my complaint; guard and preserve my life from the terror of the enemy.

²Hide me from the secret counsel and conspiracy of the ungodly, from the scheming of evildoers,

³Who whet their tongues like a sword, who aim venomous words like arrows,

⁴Who shoot from ambush at the blameless man; suddenly do they shoot at him, without self-reproach or fear.

⁵They encourage themselves in an evil purpose, they talk of laying snares secretly; they say, Who will discover us ?

⁶They think out acts of injustice and say, We have accomplished a well-devised thing! For the inward thought of each one [is unsearchable] and his heart is deep.

⁷But God will shoot an unexpected arrow at them; and suddenly shall they be wounded.

⁸And they will be made to stumble, their own tongues turning against them; all who gaze upon them will shake their heads and flee away.

[9]And all men shall [reverently] fear and be in awe; and they will declare the work of God, for they will wisely consider and acknowledge that it is His doing.

[10]The [uncompromisingly] righteous shall be glad in the Lord and shall trust and take refuge in Him; and all the upright in heart shall glory and offer praise.

PSALM 65

To the Chief Musician. A Psalm of David. A song.

[1]TO YOU belongs silence (the submissive wonder of reverence which bursts forth into praise) and praise is due and fitting to You, O God, in Zion; and to You shall the vow be performed.

[2]O You Who hear prayer, to You shall all flesh come.

[3]Iniquities and much varied guilt prevail against me; [yet] as for our transgressions, You forgive and purge them away [make atonement for them and cover them out of Your sight]!

[4]Blessed (happy, fortunate, to be envied) is the man whom You choose and cause to come near, that he may dwell in Your courts! We shall be satisfied with the goodness of Your house, Your holy temple.

[5]By fearful and glorious things [that terrify the wicked but make the godly sing praises] do You answer us in righteousness (rightness and justice), O God of our salvation, You Who are the confidence and hope of all the ends of the earth and of those far off on the seas;

[6]Who by [Your] might have founded the mountains, being girded with power,

[7]Who still the roaring of the seas, the roaring of their waves, and the tumult of the peoples,

[8]So that those who dwell in earth's farthest parts are afraid of [nature's] signs of Your presence. You make the places where morning and evening have birth to shout for joy.

[9]You visit the earth and saturate it with water; You greatly enrich it; the river of God is full of water; You provide them with grain when You have so prepared the earth.

[10]You water the field's furrows abundantly, You settle the ridges of it; You make the soil soft with showers, blessing the sprouting of its vegetation.

[11]You crown the year with Your bounty and goodness, and the tracks of Your [chariot wheels] drip with fatness.

¹²The [luxuriant] pastures in the uncultivated country drip [with moisture], and the hills gird themselves with joy.

¹³The meadows are clothed with flocks, the valleys also are covered with grain; they shout for joy and sing together.

PSALM 66
To the Chief Musician. A song. A Psalm.

¹MAKE A joyful noise unto God, all the earth;

²Sing forth the honor and glory of His name; make His praise glorious!

³Say to God, How awesome and fearfully glorious are Your works! Through the greatness of Your power shall Your enemies submit themselves to You [with feigned and reluctant obedience].

⁴All the earth shall bow down to You and sing [praises] to You; they shall praise Your name in song. Selah [pause, and calmly think of that]!

⁵Come and see the works of God; see how [to save His people He smites their foes; He is] terrible in His doings toward the children of men.

⁶He turned the sea into dry land, they crossed through the river on foot; there did we rejoice in Him.

⁷He rules by His might forever, His eyes observe and keep watch over the nations; let not the rebellious exalt themselves. Selah [pause, and calmly think of that]!

⁸Bless our God, O peoples, give Him grateful thanks and make the voice of His praise be heard,

⁹Who put and kept us among the living, and has not allowed our feet to slip.

¹⁰For You, O God, have proved us; You have tried us as silver is tried, refined, and purified.

¹¹You brought us into the net (the prison fortress, the dungeon); You laid a heavy burden upon our loins.

¹²You caused men to ride over our heads [when we were prostrate]; we went through fire and through water, but You brought us out into a broad, moist place [to abundance and refreshment and the open air].

¹³I will come into Your house with burnt offerings [of entire consecration]; I will pay You my vows,

[14]Which my lips uttered and my mouth promised when I was in distress.

[15]I will offer to You burnt offerings of fat lambs, with rams consumed in sweet-smelling smoke; I will offer bullocks and he-goats. Selah [pause, and calmly think of that]!

[16]Come and hear, all you who reverently and worshipfully fear God, and I will declare what He has done for me!

[17]I cried aloud to Him; He was extolled and high praise was under my tongue.

[18]If I regard iniquity in my heart, the Lord will not hear me;

[19]But certainly God has heard me; He has given heed to the voice of my prayer.

[20]Blessed be God, Who has not rejected my prayer nor removed His mercy and loving-kindness from being [as it always is] with me.

PSALM 67

To the Chief Musician; on stringed instruments. A song.

[1]GOD BE merciful and gracious to us and bless us and cause His face to shine upon us and among us--Selah [pause, and calmly think of that]!--

[2]That Your way may be known upon earth, Your saving power (Your deliverances and Your salvation) among all nations.

[3]Let the peoples praise You [turn away from their idols] and give thanks to You, O God; let all the peoples praise and give thanks to You.

[4]O let the nations be glad and sing for joy, for You will judge the peoples fairly and guide, lead, or drive the nations upon earth. Selah [pause, and calmly think of that]!

[5]Let the peoples praise You [turn away from their idols] and give thanks to You, O God; let all the peoples praise and give thanks to You!

[6]The earth has yielded its harvest [evidence of God's approval]; God, even our own God, will bless us.

[7]God will bless us, and all the ends of the earth shall reverently fear Him.

PSALM 68

To the Chief Musician. A Psalm of David. A song.

¹GOD IS beginning to arise, and His enemies to scatter; let them also who hate Him flee before Him!

²As smoke is driven away, so drive them away; as wax melts before the fire, so let the wicked perish before the presence of God.

³But let the [uncompromisingly] righteous be glad; let them be in high spirits and glory before God, yes, let them [jubilantly] rejoice!

⁴Sing to God, sing praises to His name, cast up a highway for Him Who rides through the deserts--His name is the Lord--be in high spirits and glory before Him!

⁵A father of the fatherless and a judge and protector of the widows is God in His holy habitation.

⁶God places the solitary in families and gives the desolate a home in which to dwell; He leads the prisoners out to prosperity; but the rebellious dwell in a parched land.

⁷O God, when You went forth before Your people, when You marched through the wilderness--Selah [pause, and calmly think of that]!--

⁸The earth trembled, the heavens also poured down [rain] at the presence of God; yonder Sinai quaked at the presence of God, the God of Israel.

⁹You, O God, did send a plentiful rain; You did restore and confirm Your heritage when it languished and was weary.

¹⁰Your flock found a dwelling place in it; You, O God, in Your goodness did provide for the poor and needy.

¹¹The Lord gives the word [of power]; the women who bear and publish [the news] are a great host.

¹²The kings of the enemies' armies, they flee, they flee! She who tarries at home divides the spoil [left behind].

¹³Though you [the slackers] may lie among the sheepfolds [in slothful ease, yet for Israel] the wings of a dove are covered with silver, its pinions excessively green with gold [are trophies taken from the enemy].

¹⁴When the Almighty scattered kings in [the land], it was as when it snows on Zalmon [a wooded hill near Shechem].

¹⁵Is Mount Bashan the high mountain of summits, Mount Bashan [east of the Jordan] the mount of God?

¹⁶Why do you look with grudging and envy, you many-peaked mountains, at the mountain [of the city called Zion] which God has desired for His dwelling place? Yes, the Lord will dwell in it forever.

¹⁷The chariots of God are twenty thousand, even thousands upon thousands. The Lord is among them as He was in Sinai, [so also] in the Holy Place (the sanctuary in Jerusalem).

¹⁸You have ascended on high. You have led away captive a train of vanquished foes; You have received gifts of men, yes, of the rebellious also, that the Lord God might dwell there with them.

¹⁹Blessed be the Lord, Who bears our burdens and carries us day by day, even the God Who is our salvation! Selah [pause, and calmly think of that]!

²⁰God is to us a God of deliverances and salvation; and to God the Lord belongs escape from death [setting us free].

²¹But God will shatter the heads of His enemies, the hairy scalp of such a one as goes on still in his trespasses and guilty ways.

²²The Lord said, I will bring back [your enemies] from Bashan; I will bring them back from the depths of the [Red] Sea,

²³That you may crush them, dipping your foot in blood, that the tongues of your dogs may have their share from the foe.

²⁴They see Your goings, O God, even the [solemn processions] of my God, my King, into the sanctuary.

²⁵The singers go in front, the players on instruments last; between them the maidens are playing on tambourines.

²⁶Bless, give thanks, and gratefully praise God in full congregations, even the Lord, O you who are from [Jacob] the fountain of Israel.

²⁷There is little Benjamin in the lead [in the procession], the princes of Judah and their company, the princes of Zebulun, and the princes of Naphtali.

²⁸Your God has commanded your strength [your might in His service and impenetrable hardness to temptation]; O God, display Your might and strengthen what You have wrought for us!

²⁹[Out of respect] for Your temple at Jerusalem kings shall bring gifts to You.

³⁰Rebuke the wild beasts dwelling among the reeds [in Egypt], the herd of bulls (the leaders) with the calves of the peoples; trample underfoot those who lust for tribute money; scatter the peoples who delight in war.

³¹Princes shall come out of Egypt; Ethiopia shall hasten to stretch out her hands [with the offerings of submission] to God.

³²Sing to God, O kingdoms of the earth, sing praises to the Lord! Selah [pause, and calmly think of that]!

³³[Sing praises] to Him Who rides upon the heavens, the ancient heavens; behold, He sends forth His voice, His mighty voice.

³⁴Ascribe power and strength to God; His majesty is over Israel, and His strength and might are in the skies.

³⁵O God, awe-inspiring, profoundly impressive, and terrible are You out of Your holy places; the God of Israel Himself gives strength and fullness of might to His people. Blessed be God!

PSALM 69

To the Chief Musician; [set to the tune of] "Lilies."
[A Psalm] of David.

¹SAVE ME, O God, for the waters have come up to my neck [they threaten my life].

²I sink in deep mire, where there is no foothold; I have come into deep waters, where the floods overwhelm me.

³I am weary with my crying; my throat is parched; my eyes fail with waiting [hopefully] for my God.

⁴Those who hate me without cause are more than the hairs of my head; those who would cut me off and destroy me, being my enemies wrongfully, are many and mighty. I am [forced] to restore what I did not steal.

⁵O God, You know my folly and blundering; my sins and my guilt are not hidden from You.

⁶Let not those who wait and hope and look for You, O Lord of hosts, be put to shame through me; let not those who seek and inquire for and require You [as their vital necessity] be brought to confusion and dishonor through me, O God of Israel.

⁷Because for Your sake I have borne taunt and reproach; confusion and shame have covered my face.

⁸I have become a stranger to my brethren, and an alien to my mother's children.

⁹For zeal for Your house has eaten me up, and the reproaches and insults of those who reproach and insult You have fallen upon me.

¹⁰When I wept and humbled myself with fasting, I was jeered at and humiliated;

¹¹When I made sackcloth my clothing, I became a byword (an object of scorn) to them.

¹²They who sit in [the city's] gate talk about me, and I am the song of the drunkards.

¹³But as for me, my prayer is to You, O Lord. At an acceptable and opportune time, O God, in the multitude of Your mercy and the abundance of Your loving-kindness hear me, and in the truth and faithfulness of Your salvation answer me.

¹⁴Rescue me out of the mire, and let me not sink; let me be delivered from those who hate me and from out of the deep waters.

¹⁵Let not the floodwaters overflow and overwhelm me, neither let the deep swallow me up nor the [dug] pit [with water perhaps in the bottom] close its mouth over me.

¹⁶Hear and answer me, O Lord, for Your loving-kindness is sweet and comforting; according to Your plenteous tender mercy and steadfast love turn to me.

¹⁷Hide not Your face from Your servant, for I am in distress; O answer me speedily!

¹⁸Draw close to me and redeem me; ransom and set me free because of my enemies [lest they glory in my prolonged distress]!

¹⁹You know my reproach and my shame and my dishonor; my adversaries are all before You [fully known to You].

²⁰Insults and reproach have broken my heart; I am full of heaviness and I am distressingly sick. I looked for pity, but there was none, and for comforters, but I found none.

²¹They gave me also gall [poisonous and bitter] for my food, and in my thirst they gave me vinegar (a soured wine) to drink.

²²Let their own table [with all its abundance and luxury] become a snare to them; and when they are secure in peace [or at their sacrificial feasts, let it become] a trap to them.

²³Let their eyes be darkened so that they cannot see, and make their loins tremble continually [from terror, dismay, and feebleness].

²⁴Pour out Your indignation upon them, and let the fierceness of Your burning anger catch up with them.

²⁵Let their habitation and their encampment be a desolation; let no one dwell in their tents.

²⁶For they pursue and persecute him whom You have smitten, and they gossip about those whom You have wounded, [adding] to their grief and pain.

²⁷Let one [unforgiven] perverseness and iniquity accumulate upon another for them [in Your book], and let them not come into Your righteousness or be justified and acquitted by You.

²⁸Let them be blotted out of the book of the living and the book of life and not be enrolled among the righteous (those in right standing with God).

²⁹But I am poor, sorrowful, and in pain; let Your salvation, O God, set me up on high.

³⁰I will praise the name of God with a song and will magnify Him with thanksgiving,

³¹And it will please the Lord better than an ox or a bullock that has horns and hoofs.

³²The humble shall see it and be glad; you who seek God, inquiring for and requiring Him [as your first need], let your hearts revive and live!

³³For the Lord hears the poor and needy and despises not His prisoners (His miserable and wounded ones).

³⁴Let heaven and earth praise Him, the seas and everything that moves in them.

³⁵For God will save Zion and rebuild the cities of Judah; and [His servants] shall remain and dwell there and have it in their possession;

³⁶The children of His servants shall inherit it, and those who love His name shall dwell in it.

PSALM 70

To the Chief Musician. [A Psalm] of David, to bring to remembrance or make memorial.

¹MAKE HASTE, O God, to deliver me; make haste to help me, O Lord!

²Let them be put to shame and confounded that seek and demand my life; let them be turned backward and brought to confusion and dishonor who desire and delight in my hurt.

³Let them be turned back and appalled because of their shame and disgrace who say, Aha, aha!

⁴May all those who seek, inquire of and for You, and require You [as their vital need] rejoice and be glad in You; and may those who love Your salvation say continually, Let God be magnified!

⁵But I am poor and needy; hasten to me, O God! You are my Help and my Deliverer; O Lord, do not tarry!

PSALM 71

¹IN YOU, O Lord, do I put my trust and confidently take refuge; let me never be put to shame or confusion!

²Deliver me in Your righteousness and cause me to escape; bow down Your ear to me and save me!

³Be to me a rock of refuge in which to dwell, and a sheltering stronghold to which I may continually resort, which You have appointed to save me, for You are my Rock and my Fortress.

⁴Rescue me, O my God, out of the hand of the wicked, out of the grasp of the unrighteous and ruthless man.

⁵For You are my hope; O Lord God, You are my trust from my youth and the source of my confidence.

⁶Upon You have I leaned and relied from birth; You are He Who took me from my mother's womb and You have been my benefactor from that day. My praise is continually of You.

⁷I am as a wonder and surprise to many, but You are my strong refuge.

⁸My mouth shall be filled with Your praise and with Your honor all the day.

⁹Cast me not off nor send me away in the time of old age; forsake me not when my strength is spent and my powers fail.

¹⁰For my enemies talk against me; those who watch for my life consult together,

¹¹Saying, God has forsaken him; pursue and persecute and take him, for there is none to deliver him.

¹²O God, be not far from me! O my God, make haste to help me!

¹³Let them be put to shame and consumed who are adversaries to my life; let them be covered with reproach, scorn, and dishonor who seek and require my hurt.

¹⁴But I will hope continually, and will praise You yet more and more.

¹⁵My mouth shall tell of Your righteous acts and of Your deeds of salvation all the day, for their number is more than I know.

¹⁶I will come in the strength and with the mighty acts of the Lord God; I will mention and praise Your righteousness, even Yours alone.

¹⁷O God, You have taught me from my youth, and hitherto have I declared Your wondrous works.

¹⁸Yes, even when I am old and gray-headed, O God, forsake me not, [but keep me alive] until I have declared Your mighty strength to [this] generation, and Your might and power to all that are to come.

¹⁹Your righteousness also, O God, is very high [reaching to the heavens], You Who have done great things; O God, who is like You, or who is Your equal?

²⁰You Who have shown us [all] troubles great and sore will quicken us again and will bring us up again from the depths of the earth.

²¹Increase my greatness (my honor) and turn and comfort me.

²²I will also praise You with the harp, even Your truth and faithfulness, O my God; unto You will I sing praises with the lyre, O Holy One of Israel.

²³My lips shall shout for joy when I sing praises to You, and my inner being, which You have redeemed.

²⁴My tongue also shall talk of Your righteousness all the day long; for they are put to shame, for they are confounded, who seek and demand my hurt.

PSALM 72
[A Psalm] for Solomon.

¹GIVE THE king [knowledge of] Your [way of] judging, O God, and [the spirit of] Your righteousness to the king's son [to control all his actions].

²Let him judge and govern Your people with righteousness, and Your poor and afflicted ones with judgment and justice.

³The mountains shall bring peace to the people, and the hills, through [the general establishment of] righteousness.

⁴May he judge and defend the poor of the people, deliver the children of the needy, and crush the oppressor,

⁵So that they may revere and fear You while the sun and moon endure, throughout all generations.

⁶May he [Solomon as a type of King David's greater Son] be like rain that comes down upon the mown grass, like showers that water the earth.

⁷In His [Christ's] days shall the [uncompromisingly] righteous flourish and peace abound till there is a moon no longer.

⁸He [Christ] shall have dominion also from sea to sea and from the River [Euphrates] to the ends of the earth.

⁹Those who dwell in the wilderness shall bow before Him and His enemies shall lick the dust.

¹⁰The kings of Tarshish and of the coasts shall bring offerings; the kings of Sheba and Seba shall offer gifts.

¹¹Yes, all kings shall fall down before Him, all nations shall serve Him.

¹²For He delivers the needy when he calls out, the poor also and him who has no helper.

¹³He will have pity on the poor and weak and needy and will save the lives of the needy.

¹⁴He will redeem their lives from oppression and fraud and violence, and precious and costly shall their blood be in His sight.

¹⁵And He shall live; and to Him shall be given gold of Sheba; prayer also shall be made for Him and through Him continually, and they shall bless and praise Him all the day long.

¹⁶There shall be abundance of grain in the soil upon the top of the mountains [the least fruitful places in the land]; the fruit of it shall wave like [the forests of] Lebanon, and [the inhabitants of] the city shall flourish like grass of the earth.

¹⁷His name shall endure forever; His name shall continue as long as the sun [indeed, His name continues before the sun]. And men shall be blessed and bless themselves by Him; all nations shall call Him blessed!

¹⁸Blessed be the Lord God, the God of Israel, Who alone does wondrous things!

¹⁹Blessed be His glorious name forever; let the whole earth be filled with His glory! Amen and Amen!

²⁰The prayers of David son of Jesse are ended.

PSALM 73

A Psalm of Asaph.

¹TRULY GOD is [only] good to Israel, even to those who are upright and pure in heart.

²But as for me, my feet were almost gone, my steps had well-nigh slipped.

³For I was envious of the foolish and arrogant when I saw the prosperity of the wicked.

⁴For they suffer no violent pangs in their death, but their strength is firm.

⁵They are not in trouble as other men; neither are they smitten and plagued like other men.

⁶Therefore pride is about their necks like a chain; violence covers them like a garment [like a long, luxurious robe].

⁷Their eyes stand out with fatness, they have more than heart could wish; and the imaginations of their minds overflow [with follies].

⁸They scoff, and wickedly utter oppression; they speak loftily [from on high, maliciously and blasphemously].

⁹They set their mouths against and speak down from heaven, and their tongues swagger through the earth [invading even heaven with blasphemy and smearing earth with slanders].

¹⁰Therefore His people return here, and waters of a full cup [offered by the wicked] are [blindly] drained by them.

¹¹And they say, How does God know? Is there knowledge in the Most High?

¹²Behold, these are the ungodly, who always prosper and are at ease in the world; they increase in riches.

¹³Surely then in vain have I cleansed my heart and washed my hands in innocency.

¹⁴For all the day long have I been smitten and plagued, and chastened every morning.

¹⁵Had I spoken thus [and given expression to my feelings], I would have been untrue and have dealt treacherously against the generation of Your children.

¹⁶But when I considered how to understand this, it was too great an effort for me and too painful

¹⁷Until I went into the sanctuary of God; then I understood [for I considered] their end.

¹⁸[After all] You do set the [wicked] in slippery places; You cast them down to ruin and destruction.

¹⁹How they become a desolation in a moment! They are utterly consumed with terrors!

²⁰As a dream [which seems real] until one awakens, so, O Lord, when You arouse Yourself [to take note of the wicked], You will despise their outward show.

²¹For my heart was grieved, embittered, and in a state of ferment, and I was pricked in my heart [as with the sharp fang of an adder].

²²So foolish, stupid, and brutish was I, and ignorant; I was like a beast before You.

²³Nevertheless I am continually with You; You do hold my right hand.

²⁴You will guide me with Your counsel, and afterward receive me to honor and glory.

²⁵Whom have I in heaven but You? And I have no delight or desire on earth besides You.

²⁶My flesh and my heart may fail, but God is the Rock and firm Strength of my heart and my Portion forever.

²⁷For behold, those who are far from You shall perish; You will destroy all who are false to You and like [spiritual] harlots depart from You.

²⁸But it is good for me to draw near to God; I have put my trust in the Lord God and made Him my refuge, that I may tell of all Your works.

PSALM 74

A skillful song, or a didactic or reflective poem,
of Asaph.

¹O GOD, why do You cast us off forever? Why does Your anger burn and smoke against the sheep of Your pasture?

²[Earnestly] remember Your congregation which You have acquired of old, which You have redeemed to be the tribe of Your heritage; remember Mount Zion, where You have dwelt.

³Direct Your feet [quickly] to the perpetual ruins and desolations; the foe has devastated and desecrated everything in the sanctuary.

⁴In the midst of Your Holy Place Your enemies have roared [their battle cry]; they set up their own [idol] emblems for signs [of victory].

⁵They seemed like men who lifted up axes upon a thicket of trees to make themselves a record.

⁶And then all the carved wood of the Holy Place they broke down with hatchets and hammers.

⁷They have set Your sanctuary on fire; they have profaned the dwelling place of Your Name by casting it to the ground.

⁸They said in their hearts, Let us make havoc [of such places] altogether. They have burned up all God's meetinghouses in the land.

⁹We do not see our symbols; there is no longer any prophet, neither does any among us know for how long.

¹⁰O God, how long is the adversary to scoff and reproach? Is the enemy to blaspheme and revile Your name forever?

¹¹Why do You hold back Your hand, even Your right hand? Draw it out of Your bosom and consume them [make an end of them]!

¹²Yet God is my King of old, working salvation in the midst of the earth.

¹³You did divide the [Red] Sea by Your might; You broke the heads of the [Egyptian] dragons in the waters.

¹⁴You crushed the heads of Leviathan (Egypt); You did give him as food for the creatures inhabiting the wilderness.

¹⁵You did cleave open [the rock bringing forth] fountains and streams; You dried up mighty, ever-flowing rivers (the Jordan).

¹⁶The day is Yours, the night also is Yours; You have established the [starry] light and the sun.

¹⁷You have fixed all the borders of the earth [the divisions of land and sea and of the nations]; You have made summer and winter. [Acts 17:26.]

¹⁸[Earnestly] remember how the enemy has scoffed, O Lord, and reproached You, and how a foolish and impious people has blasphemed Your name.

¹⁹Oh, do not deliver the life of your turtledove to the wild beast (to the greedy multitude); forget not the life [of the multitude] of Your poor forever.

²⁰Have regard for the covenant [You made with Abraham], for the dark places of the land are full of the habitations of violence.

²¹Oh, let not the downtrodden return in shame; let the oppressed and needy praise Your name.

²²Arise, O God, plead Your own cause; remember [earnestly] how the foolish and impious man scoffs and reproaches You day after day and all day long.

²³Do not forget the [clamoring] voices of Your adversaries, the tumult of those who rise up against You, which ascends continually.

PSALM 75

To the Chief Musician; [set to the tune of] "Do Not Destroy." A Psalm of Asaph. A song.

¹WE GIVE praise and thanks to You, O God, we praise and give thanks; Your wondrous works declare that Your Name is near and they who invoke Your Name rehearse Your wonders.

²When the proper time has come [for executing My judgments], I will judge uprightly [says the Lord].

³When the earth totters, and all the inhabitants of it, it is I Who will poise and keep steady its pillars. Selah [pause, and calmly think of that]!

⁴I said to the arrogant and boastful, Deal not arrogantly [do not boast]; and to the wicked, Lift not up the horn [of personal aggrandizement].

⁵Lift not up your [aggressive] horn on high, speak not with a stiff neck and insolent arrogance.

⁶For not from the east nor from the west nor from the south come promotion and lifting up.

⁷But God is the Judge! He puts down one and lifts up another.

⁸For in the hand of the Lord there is a cup [of His wrath], and the wine foams and is red, well mixed; and He pours out from it, and all the wicked of the earth must drain it and drink its dregs.

⁹But I will declare and rejoice forever; I will sing praises to the God of Jacob.

¹⁰All the horns of the ungodly also will I cut off [says the Lord], but the horns of the [uncompromisingly] righteous shall be exalted.

PSALM 76

To the Chief Musician; on stringed instruments.
A Psalm of Asaph. A song.

¹IN JUDAH God is known and renowned; His name is highly praised and is great in Israel.

²In [Jeru]Salem also is His tabernacle, and His dwelling place is in Zion.

³There He broke the bow's flashing arrows, the shield, the sword, and the weapons of war. Selah [pause, and calmly think of that]!

⁴Glorious and excellent are You from the mountains of prey [splendid and majestic, more than the everlasting mountains].

⁵The stouthearted are stripped of their spoil, they have slept the sleep [of death]; and none of the men of might could raise their hands.

⁶At Your rebuke, O God of Jacob, both chariot [rider] and horse are cast into a dead sleep [of death].

⁷You, even You, are to be feared [with awe and reverence]! Who may stand in Your presence when once Your anger is roused?

⁸You caused sentence to be heard from heaven; the earth feared and was still--

⁹When God arose to [establish] judgment, to save all the meek and oppressed of the earth. Selah [pause, and calmly think of that]!

¹⁰Surely the wrath of man shall praise You; the remainder of wrath shall You restrain and gird and arm Yourself with it.

¹¹Vow and pay to the Lord your God; let all who are round about Him bring presents to Him Who ought to be [reverently] feared.

¹²He will cut off the spirit [of pride and fury] of princes; He is terrible to the [ungodly] kings of the earth.

PSALM 77

To the Chief Musician; after the manner of Jeduthun [one of David's three chief musicians, founder of an official musical family]. A Psalm of Asaph.

¹I WILL cry to God with my voice, even to God with my voice, and He will give ear and hearken to me.

²In the day of my trouble I seek (inquire of and desperately require) the Lord; in the night my hand is stretched out [in prayer] without slacking up; I refuse to be comforted.

³I [earnestly] remember God; I am disquieted and I groan; I muse in prayer, and my spirit faints [overwhelmed]. Selah [pause, and calmly think of that]!

⁴You hold my eyes from closing; I am so troubled that I cannot speak.

⁵I consider the days of old, the years of bygone times [of prosperity].

⁶I call to remembrance my song in the night; with my heart I meditate and my spirit searches diligently:

⁷Will the Lord cast off forever? And will He be favorable no more?

⁸Have His mercy and loving-kindness ceased forever? Have His promises ended for all time?

⁹Has God [deliberately] abandoned or forgotten His graciousness? Has He in anger shut up His compassion? Selah [pause, and calmly think of that]!

¹⁰And I say, This [apparent desertion of Israel by God] is my appointed lot and trial, but I will recall the years of the right hand of the Most High [in loving-kindness extended toward us], for this is my grief, that the right hand of the Most High changes.

¹¹I will [earnestly] recall the deeds of the Lord; yes, I will [earnestly] remember the wonders [You performed for our fathers] of old.

¹²I will meditate also upon all Your works and consider all Your [mighty] deeds.

¹³Your way, O God, is in the sanctuary [in holiness, away from sin and guilt]. Who is a great God like our God?

¹⁴You are the God Who does wonders; You have demonstrated Your power among the peoples.

¹⁵You have with Your [mighty] arm redeemed Your people, the sons of Jacob and Joseph. Selah [pause, and calmly think of that]!

¹⁶When the waters [at the Red Sea and the Jordan] saw You, O God, they were afraid; the deep shuddered also, for [all] the waters saw You.

¹⁷The clouds poured down water, the skies sent out a sound [of rumbling thunder]; Your arrows went forth [in forked lightning].

¹⁸The voice of Your thunder was in the whirlwind, the lightnings illumined the world; the earth trembled and shook.

¹⁹Your way [in delivering Your people] was through the sea, and Your paths through the great waters, yet Your footsteps were not traceable, but were obliterated.

²⁰You led Your people like a flock by the hand of Moses and Aaron.

PSALM 78

A skillful song, or a didactic or reflective poem,
of Asaph.

¹GIVE EAR, O my people, to my teaching; incline your ears to the words of my mouth.

²I will open my mouth in a parable (in instruction by numerous examples); I will utter dark sayings of old [that hide important truth]--

³Which we have heard and known, and our fathers have told us.

⁴We will not hide them from their children, but we will tell to the generation to come the praiseworthy deeds of the Lord, and His might, and the wonderful works that He has performed.

⁵For He established a testimony (an express precept) in Jacob and appointed a law in Israel, commanding our fathers that they should make [the great facts of God's dealings with Israel] known to their children,

⁶That the generation to come might know them, that the children still to be born might arise and recount them to their children,

⁷That they might set their hope in God and not forget the works of God, but might keep His commandments.

⁸And might not be as their fathers--a stubborn and rebellious generation, a generation that set not their hearts aright nor prepared their hearts to know God, and whose spirits were not steadfast and faithful to God.

⁹The children of Ephraim were armed and carrying bows, yet they turned back in the day of battle.

¹⁰They kept not the covenant of God and refused to walk according to His law

¹¹And forgot His works and His wonders that He had shown them.

¹²Marvelous things did He in the sight of their fathers in the land of Egypt, in the field of Zoan [where Pharaoh resided].

¹³He divided the [Red] Sea and caused them to pass through it, and He made the waters stand like a heap.

¹⁴In the daytime also He led them with a [pillar of] cloud and all the night with a light of fire.

¹⁵He split rocks in the wilderness and gave them drink abundantly as out of the deep.

¹⁶He brought streams also out of the rock [at Rephidim and Kadesh] and caused waters to run down like rivers.

¹⁷Yet they still went on to sin against Him by provoking and rebelling against the Most High in the wilderness (in the land of drought).

¹⁸And they tempted God in their hearts by asking for food according to their [selfish] desire and appetite.

¹⁹Yes, they spoke against God; they said, Can God furnish [the food for] a table in the wilderness?

²⁰Behold, He did smite the rock so that waters gushed out and the streams overflowed; but can He give bread also? Can He provide flesh for His people?

²¹Therefore, when the Lord heard, He was [full of] wrath; a fire was kindled against Jacob, His anger mounted up against Israel,

²²Because in God they believed not [they relied not on Him, they adhered not to Him], and they trusted not in His salvation (His power to save).

²³Yet He commanded the clouds above and opened the doors of heaven;

²⁴And He rained down upon them manna to eat and gave them heaven's grain.

²⁵Everyone ate the bread of the mighty [man ate angels' food]; God sent them meat in abundance.

²⁶He let forth the east wind to blow in the heavens, and by His power He guided the south wind.

²⁷He rained flesh also upon them like the dust, and winged birds [quails] like the sand of the seas.

²⁸And He let [the birds] fall in the midst of their camp, round about their tents.

²⁹So they ate and were well filled; He gave them what they craved and lusted after.

³⁰But scarce had they stilled their craving, and while their meat was yet in their mouths,

³¹The wrath of God came upon them and slew the strongest and sturdiest of them and smote down Israel's chosen youth.

³²In spite of all this, they sinned still more, for they believed not in (relied not on and adhered not to Him for) His wondrous works.

³³Therefore their days He consumed like a breath [in emptiness, falsity, and futility] and their years in terror and sudden haste.

[34]When He slew [some of] them, [the remainder] inquired after Him diligently, and they repented and sincerely sought God [for a time].

[35]And they [earnestly] remembered that God was their Rock, and the Most High God their Redeemer.

[36]Nevertheless they flattered Him with their mouths and lied to Him with their tongues.

[37]For their hearts were not right or sincere with Him, neither were they faithful and steadfast to His covenant.

[38]But He, full of [merciful] compassion, forgave their iniquity and destroyed them not; yes, many a time He turned His anger away and did not stir up all His wrath and indignation.

[39]For He [earnestly] remembered that they were but flesh, a wind that goes and does not return.

[40]How often they defied and rebelled against Him in the wilderness and grieved Him in the desert!

[41]And time and again they turned back and tempted God, provoking and incensing the Holy One of Israel.

[42]They remembered not [seriously the miracles of the working of] His hand, nor the day when He delivered them from the enemy,

[43]How He wrought His miracles in Egypt and His wonders in the field of Zoan [where Pharaoh resided]

[44]And turned their rivers into blood, and their streams, so that they could not drink from them.

[45]He sent swarms of flies among them which devoured them, and frogs which destroyed them.

[46]He gave also their crops to the caterpillar and [the fruit of] their labor to the locust.

[47]He destroyed their vines with hail and their sycamore trees with frost and [great chunks of] ice.

[48]He [caused them to shut up their cattle or] gave them up also to the hail and their flocks to hot thunderbolts.

[49]He let loose upon them the fierceness of His anger, His wrath and indignation and distress, by sending [a mission of] angels of calamity and woe among them.

[50]He leveled and made a straight path for His anger; He did not spare [the Egyptians] from death but gave their beasts over to the pestilence and the life [of their eldest] over to the plague.

⁵¹He smote all the firstborn in Egypt, the chief of their strength in the tents [of the land of the sons] of Ham.

⁵²But [God] led His own people forth like sheep and guided them [with a shepherd's care] like a flock in the wilderness.

⁵³And He led them on safely and in confident trust, so that they feared not; but the sea overwhelmed their enemies.

⁵⁴And He brought them to His holy border, the border of [Canaan] His sanctuary, even to this mountain [Zion] which His right hand had acquired.

⁵⁵He drove out the nations also before [Israel] and allotted their land as a heritage, measured out and partitioned; and He made the tribes of Israel to dwell in the tents of those dispossessed.

⁵⁶Yet they tempted and provoked and rebelled against the Most High God and kept not His testimonies.

⁵⁷But they turned back and dealt unfaithfully and treacherously like their fathers; they were twisted like a warped and deceitful bow [that will not respond to the archer's aim].

⁵⁸For they provoked Him to [righteous] anger with their high places [for idol worship] and moved Him to jealousy with their graven images.

⁵⁹When God heard this, He was full of [holy] wrath; and He utterly rejected Israel, greatly abhorring and loathing [her ways],

⁶⁰So that He forsook the tabernacle at Shiloh, the tent in which He had dwelt among men [and never returned to it again],

⁶¹And delivered His strength and power (the ark of the covenant) into captivity, and His glory into the hands of the foe (the Philistines).

⁶²He gave His people over also to the sword and was wroth with His heritage [Israel].

⁶³The fire [war] devoured their young men, and their bereaved virgins were not praised in a wedding song.

⁶⁴Their priests [Hophni and Phinehas] fell by the sword, and their widows made no lamentation [for the bodies came not back from the scene of battle, and the widow of Phinehas also died that day].

⁶⁵Then the Lord awakened as from sleep, as a strong man whose consciousness of power is heightened by wine.

⁶⁶And He smote His adversaries in the back [as they fled]; He put them to lasting shame and reproach.

⁶⁷Moreover, He rejected the tent of Joseph and chose not the tribe of Ephraim [in which the tabernacle had been accustomed to stand].

⁶⁸But He chose the tribe of Judah [as Israel's leader], Mount Zion, which He loved [to replace Shiloh as His capital].

⁶⁹And He built His sanctuary [exalted] like the heights [of the heavens] and like the earth which He established forever.

⁷⁰He chose David His servant and took him from the sheepfolds;

⁷¹From tending the ewes that had their young He brought him to be the shepherd of Jacob His people, of Israel His inheritance.

⁷²So [David] was their shepherd with an upright heart; he guided them by the discernment and skillfulness [which controlled] his hands.

PSALM 79

A Psalm of Asaph.

¹O GOD, the nations have come into [the land of Your people] Your inheritance; Your sacred temple have they defiled; they have made Jerusalem heaps of ruins.

²The dead bodies of Your servants they have given as food to the birds of the heavens, the flesh of Your saints to the beasts of the earth.

³Their blood they have poured out like water round about Jerusalem, and there was none to bury them.

⁴[Because of such humiliation] we have become a taunt and reproach to our neighbors, a mocking and derision to those who are round about us.

⁵How long, O Lord? Will You be angry forever? Shall Your jealousy [which cannot endure a divided allegiance] burn like fire?

⁶Pour out Your wrath on the Gentile nations who do not acknowledge You, and upon the kingdoms that do not call on Your name.

⁷For they have devoured Jacob and laid waste his dwelling and his pasture.

⁸O do not [earnestly] remember against us the iniquities and guilt of our forefathers! Let Your compassion and tender mercy speedily come to meet us, for we are brought very low.

⁹Help us, O God of our salvation, for the glory of Your name! Deliver us, forgive us, and purge away our sins for Your name's sake.

[10]Why should the Gentile nations say, Where is their God? Let vengeance for the blood of Your servants which is poured out be known among the nations in our sight [not delaying until some future generation].

[11]Let the groaning and sighing of the prisoner come before You; according to the greatness of Your power and Your arm spare those who are appointed to die!

[12]And return into the bosom of our neighbors sevenfold the taunts with which they have taunted and scoffed at You, O Lord!

[13]Then we Your people, the sheep of Your pasture, will give You thanks forever; we will show forth and publish Your praise from generation to generation.

PSALM 80

To the Chief Musician; [set to the tune of]
"Lilies, a Testimony." A Psalm of Asaph.

[1]GIVE EAR, O Shepherd of Israel, You Who lead Joseph like a flock; You Who sit enthroned upon the cherubim [of the ark of the covenant], shine forth

[2]Before Ephraim and Benjamin and Manasseh! Stir up Your might, and come to save us!

[3]Restore us again, O God; and cause Your face to shine [in pleasure and approval on us], and we shall be saved!

[4]O Lord God of hosts, how long will You be angry with Your people's prayers?

[5]You have fed them with the bread of tears, and You have given them tears to drink in large measure.

[6]You make us a strife and scorn to our neighbors, and our enemies laugh among themselves.

[7]Restore us again, O God of hosts; and cause Your face to shine [upon us with favor as of old], and we shall be saved!

[8]You brought a vine [Israel] out of Egypt; You drove out the [heathen] nations and planted it [in Canaan].

[9]You prepared room before it, and it took deep root and it filled the land.

[10]The mountains were covered with the shadow of it, and the boughs of it were like the great cedars [cedars of God].

¹¹[Israel] sent out its boughs to the [Mediterranean] Sea and its branches to the [Euphrates] River.

¹²Why have You broken down its hedges and walls so that all who pass by pluck from its fruit?

¹³The boar out of the wood wastes it and the wild beast of the field feeds on it.

¹⁴Turn again, we beseech You, O God of hosts! Look down from heaven and see, visit, and have regard for this vine!

¹⁵[Protect and maintain] the stock which Your right hand planted, and the branch (the son) that You have reared and made strong for Yourself.

¹⁶They have burned it with fire, it is cut down; may they perish at the rebuke of Your countenance.

¹⁷Let Your hand be upon the man of Your right hand, upon the son of man whom You have made strong for Yourself.

¹⁸Then will we not depart from You; revive us (give us life) and we will call upon Your name.

¹⁹Restore us, O Lord God of hosts; cause Your face to shine [in pleasure, approval, and favor on us], and we shall be saved!

PSALM 81

To the Chief Musician; set to Philistine lute, or [possibly] a particular Gittite tune. [A Psalm] of Asaph.

¹SING ALOUD to God our Strength! Shout for joy to the God of Jacob!

²Raise a song, sound the timbrel, the sweet lyre with the harp.

³Blow the trumpet at the New Moon, at the full moon, on our feast day.

⁴For this is a statute for Israel, an ordinance of the God of Jacob.

⁵This He ordained in Joseph [the savior] for a testimony when He went out over the land of Egypt. The speech of One Whom I knew not did I hear [saying],

⁶I removed his shoulder from the burden; his hands were freed from the basket.

⁷You called in distress and I delivered you; I answered you in the secret place of thunder; I tested you at the waters of Meribah. Selah [pause, and calmly think of that]!

⁸Hear, O My people, and I will admonish you--O Israel, if you would listen to Me!

⁹There shall no strange god be among you, neither shall you worship any alien god.

¹⁰I am the Lord your God, Who brought you up out of the land of Egypt. Open your mouth wide and I will fill it.

¹¹But My people would not hearken to My voice, and Israel would have none of Me.

¹²So I gave them up to their own hearts' lust and let them go after their own stubborn will, that they might follow their own counsels.

¹³Oh, that My people would listen to Me, that Israel would walk in My ways!

¹⁴Speedily then I would subdue their enemies and turn My hand against their adversaries.

¹⁵[Had Israel listened to Me in Egypt, then] those who hated the Lord would have come cringing before Him, and their defeat would have lasted forever.

¹⁶[God] would feed [Israel now] also with the finest of the wheat; and with honey out of the rock would I satisfy you.

PSALM 82

A Psalm of Asaph.

¹GOD STANDS in the assembly [of the representatives] of God; in the midst of the magistrates or judges He gives judgment [as] among the gods.

²How long will you [magistrates or judges] judge unjustly and show partiality to the wicked? Selah [pause, and calmly think of that]!

³Do justice to the weak (poor) and fatherless; maintain the rights of the afflicted and needy.

⁴Deliver the poor and needy; rescue them out of the hand of the wicked.

⁵[The magistrates and judges] know not, neither will they understand; they walk on in the darkness [of complacent satisfaction]; all the foundations of the earth [the fundamental principles upon which rests the administration of justice] are shaking.

⁶I said, You are gods [since you judge on My behalf, as My representatives]; indeed, all of you are children of the Most High.

⁷But you shall die as men and fall as one of the princes.

⁸Arise, O God, judge the earth! For to You belong all the nations.

PSALM 83

A song. A Psalm of Asaph.

¹KEEP NOT silence, O God; hold not Your peace or be still, O God.

²For, behold, Your enemies are in tumult, and those who hate You have raised their heads.

³They lay crafty schemes against Your people and consult together against Your hidden and precious ones.

⁴They have said, Come, and let us wipe them out as a nation; let the name of Israel be in remembrance no more.

⁵For they have consulted together with one accord and one heart; against You they make a covenant--

⁶The tents of Edom and the Ishmaelites, of Moab and the Hagrites,

⁷Gebal and Ammon and Amalek, the Philistines, with the inhabitants of Tyre.

⁸Assyria also has joined with them; they have helped the children of Lot [the Ammonites and the Moabites] and have been an arm to them. Selah [pause, and calmly think of that]!

⁹Do to them as [You did to] the Midianites, as to Sisera and Jabin at the brook of Kishon,

¹⁰Who perished at Endor, who became like manure for the earth.

¹¹Make their nobles like Oreb and Zeeb, yes, all their princes as Zebah and Zalmunna,

¹²Who say, Let us take possession for ourselves of the pastures of God.

¹³O my God, make them like whirling dust, like stubble or chaff before the wind!

¹⁴As fire consumes the forest, and as the flame sets the mountains ablaze,

¹⁵So pursue and afflict them with Your tempest and terrify them with Your tornado or hurricane.

¹⁶Fill their faces with shame, that they may seek, inquire for, and insistently require Your name, O Lord.

[17]Let them be put to shame and dismayed forever; yes, let them be put to shame and perish,

[18]That they may know that You, Whose name alone is the Lord, are the Most High over all the earth.

PSALM 84

To the Chief Musician; set to a Philistine lute, or [possibly] a
particular Gittite tune. A Psalm of the sons of Korah.

[1]HOW LOVELY are Your tabernacles, O Lord of hosts!

[2]My soul yearns, yes, even pines and is homesick for the courts of the Lord; my heart and my flesh cry out and sing for joy to the living God.

[3]Yes, the sparrow has found a house, and the swallow a nest for herself, where she may lay her young--even Your altars, O Lord of hosts, my King and my God.

[4]Blessed (happy, fortunate, to be envied) are those who dwell in Your house and Your presence; they will be singing Your praises all the day long. Selah [pause, and calmly think of that]!

[5]Blessed (happy, fortunate, to be envied) is the man whose strength is in You, in whose heart are the highways to Zion.

[6]Passing through the Valley of Weeping (Baca), they make it a place of springs; the early rain also fills [the pools] with blessings.

[7]They go from strength to strength [increasing in victorious power]; each of them appears before God in Zion.

[8]O Lord God of hosts, hear my prayer; give ear, O God of Jacob! Selah [pause, and calmly think of that]!

[9]Behold our shield [the king as Your agent], O God, and look upon the face of Your anointed!

[10]For a day in Your courts is better than a thousand [anywhere else]; I would rather be a doorkeeper and stand at the threshold in the house of my God than to dwell [at ease] in the tents of wickedness.

[11]For the Lord God is a Sun and Shield; the Lord bestows [present] grace and favor and [future] glory (honor, splendor, and heavenly bliss)! No good thing will He withhold from those who walk uprightly.

[12]O Lord of hosts, blessed (happy, fortunate, to be envied) is the man who trusts in You [leaning and believing on You, committing all and confidently looking to You, and that without fear or misgiving]!

PSALM 85

To the Chief Musician. A Psalm of the sons of Korah.

[1]LORD, YOU have [at last] been favorable and have dealt graciously with Your land [of Canaan]; You have brought back [from Babylon] the captives of Jacob.

[2]You have forgiven and taken away the iniquity of Your people, You have covered all their sin. Selah [pause, and calmly realize what that means]!

[3]You have withdrawn all Your wrath and indignation, You have turned away from the blazing anger [which You had let loose].

[4]Restore us, O God of our salvation, and cause Your anger toward us to cease [forever].

[5]Will You be angry with us forever? Will You prolong Your anger [and disfavor] and spread it out to all generations?

[6]Will You not revive us again, that Your people may rejoice in You?

[7]Show us Your mercy and loving-kindness, O Lord, and grant us Your salvation.

[8]I will listen [with expectancy] to what God the Lord will say, for He will speak peace to His people, to His saints (those who are in right standing with Him)--but let them not turn again to [self-confident] folly.

[9]Surely His salvation is near to those who reverently and worshipfully fear Him, [and is ready to be appropriated] that [the manifest presence of God, His] glory may tabernacle and abide in our land.

[10]Mercy and loving-kindness and truth have met together; righteousness and peace have kissed each other.

[11]Truth shall spring up from the earth, and righteousness shall look down from heaven.

[12]Yes, the Lord will give what is good, and our land will yield its increase.

[13]Righteousness shall go before Him and shall make His footsteps a way in which to walk.

PSALM 86

A Prayer of David.

[1]INCLINE YOUR ear, O Lord, and answer me, for I am poor and distressed, needy and desiring.

²Preserve my life, for I am godly and dedicated; O my God, save Your servant, for I trust in You [leaning and believing on You, committing all and confidently looking to You, without fear or doubt].

³Be merciful and gracious to me, O Lord, for to You do I cry all the day.

⁴Make me, Your servant, to rejoice, O Lord, for to You do I lift myself up.

⁵For You, O Lord, are good, and ready to forgive [our trespasses, sending them away, letting them go completely and forever]; and You are abundant in mercy and loving-kindness to all those who call upon You.

⁶Give ear, O Lord, to my prayer; and listen to the cry of my supplications.

⁷In the day of my trouble I will call on You, for You will answer me.

⁸There is none like unto You among the gods, O Lord, neither are their works like unto Yours.

⁹All nations whom You have made shall come and fall down before You, O Lord; and they shall glorify Your name.

¹⁰For You are great and work wonders! You alone are God.

¹¹Teach me Your way, O Lord, that I may walk and live in Your truth; direct and unite my heart [solely, reverently] to fear and honor Your name.

¹²I will confess and praise You, O Lord my God, with my whole (united) heart; and I will glorify Your name forevermore.

¹³For great is Your mercy and loving-kindness toward me; and You have delivered me from the depths of Sheol [from the exceeding depths of affliction].

¹⁴O God, the proud and insolent are risen against me; a rabble of violent and ruthless men has sought and demanded my life, and they have not set You before them.

¹⁵But You, O Lord, are a God merciful and gracious, slow to anger and abounding in mercy and loving-kindness and truth.

¹⁶O turn to me and have mercy and be gracious to me; grant strength (might and inflexibility to temptation) to Your servant and save the son of Your handmaiden.

¹⁷Show me a sign of [Your evident] goodwill and favor, that those who hate me may see it and be put to shame, because You, Lord, [will show Your approval of me when You] help and comfort me.

PSALM 87

A Psalm of the sons of Korah. A song.

¹ON THE holy hills stands the city [of Jerusalem and the temple] God founded.

²The Lord loves the gates of Zion [through which the crowds of pilgrims enter from all nations] more than all the dwellings of Jacob (Israel).

³Glorious things are spoken of you, O city of God. Selah [pause, and calmly realize what that means]!

⁴I will make mention of Rahab [the poetic name for Egypt] and Babylon as among those who know [the city of God]--behold, Philistia and Tyre, with Ethiopia (Cush)--[saying], This man was born there.

⁵Yes, of Zion it shall be said, This man and that man were born in her, for the Most High Himself will establish her.

⁶The Lord shall count, when He registers the peoples, that this man was born there. Selah [pause, and calmly think of that]!

⁷The singers as well as the players on instruments shall say, All my springs (my sources of life and joy) are in you [city of our God].

PSALM 88

A song. A Psalm of the sons of Korah. To the Chief Musician; set to chant mournfully. A didactic or reflective poem of Heman the Ezrahite.

¹O LORD, the God of my salvation, I have cried to You for help by day; at night I am in Your presence.

²Let my prayer come before You and really enter into Your presence; incline Your ear to my cry!

³For I am full of troubles, and my life draws near to Sheol (the place of the dead).

⁴I am counted among those who go down into the pit (the grave); I am like a man who has no help or strength [a mere shadow],

⁵Cast away among the dead, like the slain that lie in a [nameless] grave, whom You [seriously] remember no more, and they are cut off from Your hand.

⁶You have laid me in the depths of the lowest pit, in darkness, in the deeps.

⁷Your wrath lies hard upon me, and You have afflicted me with all Your waves. Selah [pause, and calmly think of that]!

⁸You have put my [familiar] friends far from me; You have made me an abomination to them. I am shut up, and I cannot come forth.

⁹My eye grows dim because of sorrow and affliction. Lord, I have called daily on You; I have spread forth my hands to You.

¹⁰Will You show wonders to the dead? Shall the departed arise and praise You? Selah [pause, and calmly think of that]!

¹¹Shall Your steadfast love be declared in the grave? Or Your faithfulness in Abaddon (Sheol, as a place of ruin and destruction)?

¹²Shall Your wonders be known in the dark? And Your righteousness in the place of forgetfulness [where the dead forget and are forgotten]?

¹³But to You I cry, O Lord; and in the morning shall my prayer come to meet You.

¹⁴Lord, why do You cast me off? Why do You hide Your face from me?

¹⁵I was afflicted and close to death from my youth up; while I suffer Your terrors I am distracted [I faint].

¹⁶Your fierce wrath has swept over me; Your terrors have destroyed me.

¹⁷They surround me like a flood all day long; together they have closed in upon me.

¹⁸Lover and friend have You put far from me; my familiar friends are darkness and the grave.

PSALM 89

A skillful song, or a didactic or reflective poem, of Ethan the Ezrahite.

¹I WILL sing of the mercy and loving-kindness of the Lord forever; with my mouth will I make known Your faithfulness from generation to generation.

²For I have said, Mercy and loving-kindness shall be built up forever; Your faithfulness will You establish in the very heavens [unchangeable and perpetual].

³[You have said] I have made a covenant with My chosen one, I have sworn to David My servant,

⁴Your Seed I will establish forever, and I will build up your throne for all generations. Selah [pause, and calmly think of that]!

⁵Let heaven (the angels) praise Your wonders, O Lord, Your faithfulness also in the assembly of the holy ones (the holy angels).

⁶For who in the heavens can be compared to the Lord? Who among the mighty [heavenly beings] can be likened to the Lord,

⁷A God greatly feared and revered in the council of the holy ones, and to be feared and worshipfully revered above all those who are round about Him?

⁸O Lord God of hosts, who is a mighty one like unto You, O Lord? And Your faithfulness is round about You [an essential part of You at all times].

⁹You rule the raging of the sea; when its waves arise, You still them.

¹⁰You have broken Rahab (Egypt) in pieces; with Your mighty arm You have scattered Your enemies.

¹¹The heavens are Yours, the earth also is Yours; the world and all that is in it, You have founded them.

¹²The north and the south, You have created them; Mount Tabor and Mount Hermon joyously praise Your name.

¹³You have a mighty arm; strong is Your hand, Your right hand is soaring high.

¹⁴Righteousness and justice are the foundation of Your throne; mercy and loving-kindness and truth go before Your face.

¹⁵Blessed (happy, fortunate, to be envied) are the people who know the joyful sound [who understand and appreciate the spiritual blessings symbolized by the feasts]; they walk, O Lord, in the light and favor of Your countenance!

¹⁶In Your name they rejoice all the day, and in Your righteousness they are exalted.

¹⁷For You are the glory of their strength [their proud adornment], and by Your favor our horn is exalted and we walk with uplifted faces!

¹⁸For our shield belongs to the Lord, and our king to the Holy One of Israel.

¹⁹Once You spoke in a vision to Your devoted ones and said, I have endowed one who is mighty [a hero, giving him the power to help-- to be a champion for Israel]; I have exalted one chosen from among the people.

²⁰I have found David My servant; with My holy oil have I anointed him,

²¹With whom My hand shall be established and ever abide; My arm also shall strengthen him.

²²The enemy shall not exact from him or do him violence or outwit him, nor shall the wicked afflict and humble him.

²³I will beat down his foes before his face and smite those who hate him.

²⁴My faithfulness and My mercy and loving-kindness shall be with him, and in My name shall his horn be exalted [great power and prosperity shall be conferred upon him].

²⁵I will set his hand in control also on the [Mediterranean] Sea, and his right hand on the rivers [Euphrates with its tributaries].

²⁶He shall cry to Me, You are my Father, my God, and the Rock of my salvation!

²⁷Also I will make him the firstborn, the highest of the kings of the earth.

²⁸My mercy and loving-kindness will I keep for him forevermore, and My covenant shall stand fast and be faithful with him.

²⁹His Offspring also will I make to endure forever, and his throne as the days of heaven.

³⁰If his children forsake My law and walk not in My ordinances,

³¹If they break or profane My statutes and keep not My commandments,

³²Then will I punish their transgression with the rod [of chastisement], and their iniquity with stripes.

³³Nevertheless, My loving-kindness will I not break off from him, nor allow My faithfulness to fail [to lie and be false to him].

³⁴My covenant will I not break or profane, nor alter the thing that is gone out of My lips.

³⁵Once [for all] have I sworn by My holiness, which cannot be violated; I will not lie to David:

³⁶His Offspring shall endure forever, and his throne [shall continue] as the sun before Me.

³⁷It shall be established forever as the moon, the faithful witness in the heavens. Selah [pause, and calmly think of that]!

³⁸But [in apparent contradiction to all this] You [even You the faithful Lord] have cast off and rejected; You have been full of wrath against Your anointed.

³⁹You have despised and loathed and renounced the covenant with Your servant; You have profaned his crown by casting it to the ground.

⁴⁰You have broken down all his hedges and his walls; You have brought his strongholds to ruin.

⁴¹All who pass along the road spoil and rob him; he has become the scorn and reproach of his neighbors.

⁴²You have exalted the right hand of his foes; You have made all his enemies rejoice.

⁴³Moreover, You have turned back the edge of his sword and have not made him to stand in battle.

⁴⁴You have made his glory and splendor to cease and have hurled to the ground his throne.

⁴⁵The days of his youth have You shortened; You have covered him with shame. Selah [pause, and calmly think of that]!

⁴⁶How long, O Lord? Will You hide Yourself forever? How long shall Your wrath burn like fire?

⁴⁷O [earnestly] remember how short my time is and what a mere fleeting life mine is. For what emptiness, falsity, futility, and frailty You have created all men!

⁴⁸What man can live and shall not see death, or can deliver himself from the [powerful] hand of Sheol (the place of the dead)? Selah [pause, and calmly consider that]!

⁴⁹Lord, where are Your former loving-kindnesses [shown in the reigns of David and Solomon], which You swore to David in Your faithfulness?

⁵⁰Remember, Lord, and earnestly imprint [on Your heart] the reproach of Your servants, scorned and insulted, how I bear in my bosom the reproach of all the many and mighty peoples,

⁵¹With which Your enemies have taunted, O Lord, with which they have mocked the footsteps of Your anointed.

⁵²Blessed be the Lord forevermore! Amen and Amen.

PSALM 90

A Prayer of Moses the man of God.

¹LORD, YOU have been our dwelling place and our refuge in all generations [says Moses].

²Before the mountains were brought forth or ever You had formed and given birth to the earth and the world, even from everlasting to everlasting You are God.

³You turn man back to dust and corruption, and say, Return, O sons of the earthborn [to the earth]!

⁴For a thousand years in Your sight are but as yesterday when it is past, or as a watch in the night.

⁵You carry away [these disobedient people, doomed to die within forty years] as with a flood; they are as a sleep [vague and forgotten as soon as they are gone]. In the morning they are like grass which grows up--

⁶In the morning it flourishes and springs up; in the evening it is mown down and withers.

⁷For we [the Israelites in the wilderness] are consumed by Your anger, and by Your wrath are we troubled, overwhelmed, and frightened away.

⁸Our iniquities, our secret heart and its sins [which we would so like to conceal even from ourselves], You have set in the [revealing] light of Your countenance.

⁹For all our days [out here in this wilderness, says Moses] pass away in Your wrath; we spend our years as a tale that is told [for we adults know we are doomed to die soon, without reaching Canaan].

¹⁰The days of our years are threescore years and ten (seventy years)--or even, if by reason of strength, fourscore years (eighty years); yet is their pride [in additional years] only labor and sorrow, for it is soon gone, and we fly away.

¹¹Who knows the power of Your anger? [Who worthily connects this brevity of life with Your recognition of sin?] And Your wrath, who connects it with the reverent and worshipful fear that is due You?

¹²So teach us to number our days, that we may get us a heart of wisdom.

¹³Turn, O Lord [from Your fierce anger]! How long--? Revoke Your sentence and be compassionate and at ease toward Your servants.

¹⁴O satisfy us with Your mercy and loving-kindness in the morning [now, before we are older], that we may rejoice and be glad all our days.

¹⁵Make us glad in proportion to the days in which You have afflicted us and to the years in which we have suffered evil.

[16]Let Your work [the signs of Your power] be revealed to Your servants, and Your [glorious] majesty to their children.

[17]And let the beauty and delightfulness and favor of the Lord our God be upon us; confirm and establish the work of our hands--yes, the work of our hands, confirm and establish it.

PSALM 91

[1]HE WHO dwells in the secret place of the Most High shall remain stable and fixed under the shadow of the Almighty [Whose power no foe can withstand].

[2]I will say of the Lord, He is my Refuge and my Fortress, my God; on Him I lean and rely, and in Him I [confidently] trust!

[3]For [then] He will deliver you from the snare of the fowler and from the deadly pestilence.

[4][Then] He will cover you with His pinions, and under His wings shall you trust and find refuge; His truth and His faithfulness are a shield and a buckler.

[5]You shall not be afraid of the terror of the night, nor of the arrow (the evil plots and slanders of the wicked) that flies by day,

[6]Nor of the pestilence that stalks in darkness, nor of the destruction and sudden death that surprise and lay waste at noonday.

[7]A thousand may fall at your side, and ten thousand at your right hand, but it shall not come near you.

[8]Only a spectator shall you be [yourself inaccessible in the secret place of the Most High] as you witness the reward of the wicked.

[9]Because you have made the Lord your refuge, and the Most High your dwelling place,

[10]There shall no evil befall you, nor any plague or calamity come near your tent.

[11]For He will give His angels [especial] charge over you to accompany and defend and preserve you in all your ways [of obedience and service].

[12]They shall bear you up on their hands, lest you dash your foot against a stone.

[13]You shall tread upon the lion and adder; the young lion and the serpent shall you trample underfoot.

¹⁴Because he has set his love upon Me, therefore will I deliver him; I will set him on high, because he knows and understands My name [has a personal knowledge of My mercy, love, and kindness--trusts and relies on Me, knowing I will never forsake him, no, never].

¹⁵He shall call upon Me, and I will answer him; I will be with him in trouble, I will deliver him and honor him.

¹⁶With long life will I satisfy him and show him My salvation.

PSALM 92

A Psalm. A song for the Sabbath day.

¹IT IS a good and delightful thing to give thanks to the Lord, to sing praises [with musical accompaniment] to Your name, O Most High,

²To show forth Your loving-kindness in the morning and Your faithfulness by night,

³With an instrument of ten strings and with the lute, with a solemn sound upon the lyre.

⁴For You, O Lord, have made me glad by Your works; at the deeds of Your hands I joyfully sing.

⁵How great are Your doings, O Lord! Your thoughts are very deep.

⁶A man in his rude and uncultivated state knows not, neither does a [self-confident] fool understand this:

⁷That though the wicked spring up like grass and all evildoers flourish, they are doomed to be destroyed forever.

⁸But You, Lord, are on high forever.

⁹For behold, Your adversaries, O Lord, for behold, Your enemies shall perish; all the evildoers shall be scattered.

¹⁰But my horn (emblem of excessive strength and stately grace) You have exalted like that of a wild ox; I am anointed with fresh oil.

¹¹My eye looks upon those who lie in wait for me; my ears hear the evildoers that rise up against me.

¹²The [uncompromisingly] righteous shall flourish like the palm tree [be long-lived, stately, upright, useful, and fruitful]; they shall grow like a cedar in Lebanon [majestic, stable, durable, and incorruptible].

¹³Planted in the house of the Lord, they shall flourish in the courts of our God.

[14] [Growing in grace] they shall still bring forth fruit in old age; they shall be full of sap [of spiritual vitality] and [rich in the] verdure [of trust, love, and contentment].

[15] [They are living memorials] to show that the Lord is upright and faithful to His promises; He is my Rock, and there is no unrighteousness in Him.

PSALM 93

[1] THE LORD reigns, He is clothed with majesty; the Lord is robed, He has girded Himself with strength and power; the world also is established, that it cannot be moved.

[2] Your throne is established from of old; You are from everlasting.

[3] The floods have lifted up, O Lord, the floods have lifted up their voice; the floods lift up the roaring of their waves.

[4] The Lord on high is mightier and more glorious than the noise of many waters, yes, than the mighty breakers and waves of the sea.

[5] Your testimonies are very sure; holiness [in separation from sin, with simple trust and hearty obedience] is becoming to Your house, O Lord, forever.

PSALM 94

[1] O LORD God, You to Whom vengeance belongs, O God, You to Whom vengeance belongs, shine forth!

[2] Rise up, O Judge of the earth; render to the proud a fit compensation!

[3] Lord, how long shall the wicked, how long shall the wicked triumph and exult?

[4] They pour out arrogant words, speaking hard things; all the evildoers boast loftily.

[5] They crush Your people, O Lord, and afflict Your heritage.

[6] They slay the widow and the transient stranger and murder the unprotected orphan.

[7] Yet they say, The Lord does not see, neither does the God of Jacob notice it.

[8] Consider and understand, you stupid ones among the people! And you [self-confident] fools, when will you become wise?

⁹He Who planted the ear, shall He not hear? He Who formed the eye, shall He not see?

¹⁰He Who disciplines and instructs the nations, shall He not punish, He Who teaches man knowledge?

¹¹The Lord knows the thoughts of man, that they are vain (empty and futile--only a breath).

¹²Blessed (happy, fortunate, to be envied) is the man whom You discipline and instruct, O Lord, and teach out of Your law,

¹³That You may give him power to keep himself calm in the days of adversity, until the [inevitable] pit of corruption is dug for the wicked.

¹⁴For the Lord will not cast off nor spurn His people, neither will He abandon His heritage.

¹⁵For justice will return to the [uncompromisingly] righteous, and all the upright in heart will follow it.

¹⁶Who will rise up for me against the evildoers? Who will stand up for me against the workers of iniquity?

¹⁷Unless the Lord had been my help, I would soon have dwelt in [the land where there is] silence.

¹⁸When I said, My foot is slipping, Your mercy and loving-kindness, O Lord, held me up.

¹⁹In the multitude of my [anxious] thoughts within me, Your comforts cheer and delight my soul!

²⁰Shall the throne of iniquity have fellowship with You--they who frame and hide their unrighteous doings under [the sacred name of] law?

²¹They band themselves together against the life of the righteous and condemn the innocent to death.

²²But the Lord has become my High Tower and Defense, and my God the Rock of my refuge.

²³And He will turn back upon them their own iniquity and will wipe them out by means of their own wickedness; the Lord our God will wipe them out.

PSALM 95

¹O COME, let us sing to the Lord; let us make a joyful noise to the Rock of our salvation!

²Let us come before His presence with thanksgiving; let us make a joyful noise to Him with songs of praise!

³For the Lord is a great God, and a great King above all gods.

⁴In His hand are the deep places of the earth; the heights and strength of the hills are His also.

⁵The sea is His, for He made it; and His hands formed the dry land.

⁶O come, let us worship and bow down, let us kneel before the Lord our Maker [in reverent praise and supplication].

⁷For He is our God and we are the people of His pasture and the sheep of His hand. Today, if you will hear His voice,

⁸Harden not your hearts as at Meribah and as at Massah in the day of temptation in the wilderness,

⁹When your fathers tried My patience and tested Me, proved Me, and saw My work [of judgment].

¹⁰Forty years long was I grieved and disgusted with that generation, and I said, It is a people that do err in their hearts, and they do not approve, acknowledge, or regard My ways.

¹¹Wherefore I swore in My wrath that they would not enter My rest.

PSALM 96

¹O SING to the Lord a new song; sing to the Lord, all the earth!

²Sing to the Lord, bless (affectionately praise) His name; show forth His salvation from day to day.

³Declare His glory among the nations, His marvelous works among all the peoples.

⁴For great is the Lord and greatly to be praised; He is to be reverently feared and worshiped above all [so-called] gods.

⁵For all the gods of the nations are [lifeless] idols, but the Lord made the heavens.

⁶Honor and majesty are before Him; strength and beauty are in His sanctuary.

⁷Ascribe to the Lord, O you families of the peoples, ascribe to the Lord glory and strength.

⁸Give to the Lord the glory due His name; bring an offering and come [before Him] into His courts.

⁹O worship the Lord in the beauty of holiness; tremble before and reverently fear Him, all the earth.

¹⁰Say among the nations that the Lord reigns; the world also is established, so that it cannot be moved; He shall judge and rule the people righteously and with justice.

¹¹Let the heavens be glad, and let the earth rejoice; let the sea roar, and all the things which fill it;

¹²Let the field be exultant, and all that is in it! Then shall all the trees of the wood sing for joy

¹³Before the Lord, for He comes, for He comes to judge and govern the earth! He shall judge the world with righteousness and justice and the peoples with His faithfulness and truth.

PSALM 97

¹THE LORD reigns, let the earth rejoice; let the multitude of isles and coastlands be glad!

²Clouds and darkness are round about Him [as at Sinai]; righteousness and justice are the foundation of His throne.

³Fire goes before Him and burns up His adversaries round about.

⁴His lightnings illumine the world; the earth sees and trembles.

⁵The hills melted like wax at the presence of the Lord, at the presence of the Lord of the whole earth.

⁶The heavens declare His righteousness, and all the peoples see His glory.

⁷Let all those be put to shame who serve graven images, who boast in idols. Fall prostrate before Him, all you gods.

⁸Zion heard and was glad, and the daughters of Judah rejoiced [in relief] because of Your judgments, O Lord.

⁹For You, Lord, are high above all the earth; You are exalted far above all gods.

¹⁰O you who love the Lord, hate evil; He preserves the lives of His saints (the children of God), He delivers them out of the hand of the wicked.

¹¹Light is sown for the [uncompromisingly] righteous and strewn along their pathway, and joy for the upright in heart [the irrepressible joy which comes from consciousness of His favor and protection].

¹²Rejoice in the Lord, you [consistently] righteous (upright and in right standing with God), and give thanks at the remembrance of His holiness.

PSALM 98

A Psalm.

¹O SING to the Lord a new song, for He has done marvelous things; His right hand and His holy arm have wrought salvation for Him.

²The Lord has made known His salvation; His righteousness has He openly shown in the sight of the nations.

³He has [earnestly] remembered His mercy and loving-kindness, His truth and His faithfulness toward the house of Israel; all the ends of the earth have witnessed the salvation of our God.

⁴Make a joyful noise to the Lord, all the earth; break forth and sing for joy, yes, sing praises!

⁵Sing praises to the Lord with the lyre, with the lyre and the voice of melody.

⁶With trumpets and the sound of the horn make a joyful noise before the King, the Lord!

⁷Let the sea roar, and all that fills it, the world, and those who dwell in it!

⁸Let the rivers clap their hands; together let the hills sing for joy

⁹Before the Lord, for He is coming to judge [and rule] the earth; with righteousness will He judge [and rule] the world, and the peoples with equity.

PSALM 99

¹THE LORD reigns, let the peoples tremble [with reverential fear]! He sits [enthroned] above the cherubim, let the earth quake!

²The Lord is great in Zion, and He is high above all the peoples.

³Let them confess and praise Your great name, awesome and reverence inspiring! It is holy, and holy is He!

⁴The strength of the king who loves righteousness and equity You establish in uprightness; You execute justice and righteousness in Jacob (Israel).

⁵Extol the Lord our God and worship at His footstool! Holy is He!

⁶Moses and Aaron were among His priests, and Samuel was among those who called upon His name; they called upon the Lord, and He answered them.

⁷He spoke to them in the pillar of cloud; they kept His testimonies and the statutes that He gave them.

[8]You answered them, O Lord our God; You were a forgiving God to them, although avenging their evildoing and wicked practices.

[9]Extol the Lord our God and worship at His holy hill, for the Lord our God is holy!

PSALM 100

A Psalm of thanksgiving and for the thank offering.

[1]MAKE A joyful noise to the Lord, all you lands!

[2]Serve the Lord with gladness! Come before His presence with singing!

[3]Know (perceive, recognize, and understand with approval) that the Lord is God! It is He Who has made us, not we ourselves [and we are His]! We are His people and the sheep of His pasture.

[4]Enter into His gates with thanksgiving and a thank offering and into His courts with praise! Be thankful and say so to Him, bless and affectionately praise His name!

[5]For the Lord is good; His mercy and loving-kindness are everlasting, His faithfulness and truth endure to all generations.

PSALM 101

A Psalm of David.

[1]I WILL sing of mercy and loving-kindness and justice; to You, O Lord, will I sing.

[2]I will behave myself wisely and give heed to the blameless way--O when will You come to me? I will walk within my house in integrity and with a blameless heart.

[3]I will set no base or wicked thing before my eyes. I hate the work of them who turn aside [from the right path]; it shall not grasp hold of me.

[4]A perverse heart shall depart from me; I will know no evil person or thing.

[5]Whoso privily slanders his neighbor, him will I cut off [from me]; he who has a haughty look and a proud and arrogant heart I cannot and I will not tolerate.

[6]My eyes shall [look with favor] upon the faithful of the land, that they may dwell with me; he who walks blamelessly, he shall minister to me.

⁷He who works deceit shall not dwell in my house; he who tells lies shall not continue in my presence.

⁸Morning after morning I will root up all the wicked in the land, that I may eliminate all the evildoers from the city of the Lord.

PSALM 102

A Prayer of the afflicted; when he is overwhelmed and faint and pours out his complaint to God.

¹HEAR MY prayer, O Lord, and let my cry come to You.

²Hide not Your face from me in the day when I am in distress! Incline Your ear to me; in the day when I call, answer me speedily.

³For my days consume away like smoke, and my bones burn like a firebrand or like a hearth.

⁴My heart is smitten like grass and withered, so that [in absorption] I forget to eat my food.

⁵By reason of my loud groaning [from suffering and trouble] my flesh cleaves to my bones.

⁶I am like a melancholy pelican or vulture of the wilderness; I am like a [desolate] owl of the waste places.

⁷I am sleepless and lie awake [mourning], like a bereaved sparrow alone on the housetop.

⁸My adversaries taunt and reproach me all the day; and they who are angry with me use my name as a curse.

⁹For I have eaten the ashes [in which I sat] as if they were bread and have mingled my drink with weeping

¹⁰Because of Your indignation and Your wrath, for You have taken me up and cast me away.

¹¹My days are like an evening shadow that stretches out and declines [with the sun]; and I am withered like grass.

¹²But You, O Lord, are enthroned forever; and the fame of Your name endures to all generations.

¹³You will arise and have mercy and loving-kindness for Zion, for it is time to have pity and compassion for her; yes, the set time has come.

¹⁴For Your servants take [melancholy] pleasure in the stones [of her ruins] and show pity for her dust.

¹⁵So the nations shall fear and worshipfully revere the name of the Lord, and all the kings of the earth Your glory.

¹⁶When the Lord builds up Zion, He will appear in His glory;

¹⁷He will regard the plea of the destitute and will not despise their prayer.

¹⁸Let this be recorded for the generation yet unborn, that a people yet to be created shall praise the Lord.

¹⁹For He looked down from the height of His sanctuary, from heaven did the Lord behold the earth,

²⁰To hear the sighing and groaning of the prisoner, to loose those who are appointed to death,

²¹So that men may declare the name of the Lord in Zion and His praise in Jerusalem

²²When peoples are gathered together, and the kingdoms, to worship and serve the Lord.

²³He has afflicted and weakened my strength, humbling and bringing me low [with sorrow] in the way; He has shortened my days [aging me prematurely].

²⁴I said, O my God, take me not away in the midst of my days, You Whose years continue throughout all generations.

²⁵At the beginning You existed and laid the foundations of the earth; the heavens are the work of Your hands.

²⁶They shall perish, but You shall remain and endure; yes, all of them shall wear out and become old like a garment. Like clothing You shall change them, and they shall be changed and pass away.

²⁷But You remain the same, and Your years shall have no end.

²⁸The children of Your servants shall dwell safely and continue, and their descendants shall be established before You.

PSALM 103
[A Psalm] of David.

¹BLESS (AFFECTIONATELY, gratefully praise) the Lord, O my soul; and all that is [deepest] within me, bless His holy name!

²Bless (affectionately, gratefully praise) the Lord, O my soul, and forget not [one of] all His benefits--

³Who forgives [every one of] all your iniquities, Who heals [each one of] all your diseases,

⁴Who redeems your life from the pit and corruption, Who beautifies, dignifies, and crowns you with loving-kindness and tender mercy;

⁵Who satisfies your mouth [your necessity and desire at your personal age and situation] with good so that your youth, renewed, is like the eagle's [strong, overcoming, soaring]!

⁶The Lord executes righteousness and justice [not for me only, but] for all who are oppressed.

⁷He made known His ways [of righteousness and justice] to Moses, His acts to the children of Israel.

⁸The Lord is merciful and gracious, slow to anger and plenteous in mercy and loving-kindness.

⁹He will not always chide or be contending, neither will He keep His anger forever or hold a grudge.

¹⁰He has not dealt with us after our sins nor rewarded us according to our iniquities.

¹¹For as the heavens are high above the earth, so great are His mercy and loving-kindness toward those who reverently and worshipfully fear Him.

¹²As far as the east is from the west, so far has He removed our transgressions from us.

¹³As a father loves and pities his children, so the Lord loves and pities those who fear Him [with reverence, worship, and awe].

¹⁴For He knows our frame, He [earnestly] remembers and imprints [on His heart] that we are dust.

¹⁵As for man, his days are as grass; as a flower of the field, so he flourishes.

¹⁶For the wind passes over it and it is gone, and its place shall know it no more.

¹⁷But the mercy and loving-kindness of the Lord are from everlasting to everlasting upon those who reverently and worshipfully fear Him, and His righteousness is to children's children--

¹⁸To such as keep His covenant [hearing, receiving, loving, and obeying it] and to those who [earnestly] remember His commandments to do them [imprinting them on their hearts].

¹⁹The Lord has established His throne in the heavens, and His kingdom rules over all.

²⁰Bless (affectionately, gratefully praise) the Lord, you His angels, you mighty ones who do His commandments, hearkening to the voice of His word.

²¹Bless (affectionately, gratefully praise) the Lord, all you His hosts, you His ministers who do His pleasure.

²²Bless the Lord, all His works in all places of His dominion; bless (affectionately, gratefully praise) the Lord, O my soul!

PSALM 104

¹BLESS (AFFECTIONATELY, gratefully praise) the Lord, O my soul! O Lord my God, You are very great! You are clothed with honor and majesty--

²[You are the One] Who covers Yourself with light as with a garment, Who stretches out the heavens like a curtain or a tent,

³Who lays the beams of the upper room of His abode in the waters [above the firmament], Who makes the clouds His chariot, Who walks on the wings of the wind,

⁴Who makes winds His messengers, flames of fire His ministers.

⁵You laid the foundations of the earth, that it should not be moved forever.

⁶You covered it with the deep as with a garment; the waters stood above the mountains.

⁷At Your rebuke they fled; at the voice of Your thunder they hastened away.

⁸The mountains rose, the valleys sank down to the place which You appointed for them.

⁹You have set a boundary [for the waters] which they may not pass over, that they turn not again to deluge the earth.

¹⁰He sends forth springs into the valleys; their waters run among the mountains.

¹¹They give drink to every [wild] beast of the field; the wild asses quench their thirst there.

¹²Beside them the birds of the heavens have their nests; they sing among the branches.

¹³He waters the mountains from His upper rooms; the earth is satisfied and abounds with the fruit of His works.

¹⁴He causes vegetation to grow for the cattle, and all that the earth produces for man to cultivate, that he may bring forth food out of the earth--

¹⁵And wine that gladdens the heart of man, to make his face shine more than oil, and bread to support, refresh, and strengthen man's heart.

[16]The trees of the Lord are watered abundantly and are filled with sap, the cedars of Lebanon which He has planted,

[17]Where the birds make their nests; as for the stork, the fir trees are her house.

[18]The high mountains are for the wild goats; the rocks are a refuge for the conies and badgers.

[19][The Lord] appointed the moon for the seasons; the sun knows [the exact time of] its setting.

[20]You [O Lord] make darkness and it becomes night, in which creeps forth every wild beast of the forest.

[21]The young lions roar after their prey and seek their food from God.

[22]When the sun arises, they withdraw themselves and lie down in their dens.

[23]Man goes forth to his work and remains at his task until evening.

[24]O Lord, how many and varied are Your works! In wisdom have You made them all; the earth is full of Your riches and Your creatures.

[25]Yonder is the sea, great and wide, in which are swarms of innumerable creeping things, creatures both small and great.

[26]There go the ships of the sea, and Leviathan (the sea monster), which You have formed to sport in it.

[27]These all wait and are dependent upon You, that You may give them their food in due season.

[28]When You give it to them, they gather it up; You open Your hand, and they are filled with good things.

[29]When You hide Your face, they are troubled and dismayed; when You take away their breath, they die and return to their dust.

[30]When You send forth Your Spirit and give them breath, they are created, and You replenish the face of the ground.

[31]May the glory of the Lord endure forever; may the Lord rejoice in His works--

[32]Who looks on the earth, and it quakes and trembles, Who touches the mountains, and they smoke!

[33]I will sing to the Lord as long as I live; I will sing praise to my God while I have any being.

[34]May my meditation be sweet to Him; as for me, I will rejoice in the Lord.

³⁵Let sinners be consumed from the earth, and let the wicked be no more. Bless (affectionately, gratefully praise) the Lord, O my soul! Praise the Lord!

PSALM 105

¹O GIVE thanks unto the Lord, call upon His name, make known His doings among the peoples!

²Sing to Him, sing praises to Him; meditate on and talk of all His marvelous deeds and devoutly praise them.

³Glory in His holy name; let the hearts of those rejoice who seek and require the Lord [as their indispensable necessity].

⁴Seek, inquire of and for the Lord, and crave Him and His strength (His might and inflexibility to temptation); seek and require His face and His presence [continually] evermore.

⁵[Earnestly] remember the marvelous deeds that He has done, His miracles and wonders, the judgments and sentences which He pronounced [upon His enemies, as in Egypt].

⁶O you offspring of Abraham His servant, you children of Jacob, His chosen ones,

⁷He is the Lord our God; His judgments are in all the earth.

⁸He is [earnestly] mindful of His covenant and forever it is imprinted on His heart, the word which He commanded and established to a thousand generations,

⁹The covenant which He made with Abraham, and His sworn promise to Isaac,

¹⁰Which He confirmed to Jacob as a statute, to Israel as an everlasting covenant,

¹¹Saying, Unto you will I give the land of Canaan as your measured portion, possession, and inheritance.

¹²When they were but a few men in number, in fact, very few, and were temporary residents and strangers in it,

¹³When they went from one nation to another, from one kingdom to another people,

¹⁴He allowed no man to do them wrong; in fact, He reproved kings for their sakes,

¹⁵Saying, Touch not My anointed, and do My prophets no harm.

[16]Moreover, He called for a famine upon the land [of Egypt]; He cut off every source of bread.

[17]He sent a man before them, even Joseph, who was sold as a servant.

[18]His feet they hurt with fetters; he was laid in chains of iron and his soul entered into the iron,

[19]Until his word [to his cruel brothers] came true, until the word of the Lord tried and tested him.

[20]The king sent and loosed him, even the ruler of the peoples, and let him go free.

[21]He made Joseph lord of his house and ruler of all his substance,

[22]To bind his princes at his pleasure and teach his elders wisdom.

[23]Israel also came into Egypt; and Jacob sojourned in the land of Ham.

[24]There [the Lord] greatly increased His people and made them stronger than their oppressors.

[25]He turned the hearts [of the Egyptians] to hate His people, to deal craftily with His servants.

[26]He sent Moses His servant, and Aaron, whom He had chosen.

[27]They showed His signs among them, wonders and miracles in the land of Ham (Egypt).

[28]He sent [thick] darkness and made the land dark, and they [God's two servants] rebelled not against His word.

[29]He turned [Egypt's] waters into blood and caused their fish to die.

[30]Their land brought forth frogs in abundance, even in the chambers of their kings.

[31]He spoke, and there came swarms of beetles and flies and mosquitoes and lice in all their borders.

[32]He gave them hail for rain, with lightning like flaming fire in their land.

[33]He smote their vines also and their fig trees and broke the [ice-laden] trees of their borders.

[34]He spoke, and the locusts came, and the grasshoppers, and that without number,

[35]And ate up all the vegetation in their land and devoured the fruit of their ground.

[36]He smote also all the firstborn in their land, the beginning and chief substance of all their strength.

37He brought [Israel] forth also with silver and gold, and there was not one feeble person among their tribes.

38Egypt was glad when they departed, for the fear of them had fallen upon the people.

39The Lord spread a cloud for a covering [by day], and a fire to give light in the night.

40[The Israelites] asked, and He brought quails and satisfied them with the bread of heaven.

41He opened the rock, and water gushed out; it ran in the dry places like a river.

42For He [earnestly] remembered His holy word and promise to Abraham His servant.

43And He brought forth His people with joy, and His chosen ones with gladness and singing,

44And gave them the lands of the nations [of Canaan], and they reaped the fruits of those peoples' labor,

45That they might observe His statutes and keep His laws [hearing, receiving, loving, and obeying them]. Praise the Lord! (Hallelujah!)

PSALM 106

1PRAISE THE Lord! (Hallelujah!) O give thanks to the Lord, for He is good; for His mercy and loving-kindness endure forever!

2Who can put into words and tell the mighty deeds of the Lord? Or who can show forth all the praise [that is due Him]?

3Blessed (happy, fortunate, to be envied) are those who observe justice [treating others fairly] and who do right and are in right standing with God at all times.

4[Earnestly] remember me, O Lord, when You favor Your people! O visit me also when You deliver them, and grant me Your salvation!--

5That I may see and share the welfare of Your chosen ones, that I may rejoice in the gladness of Your nation, that I may glory with Your heritage.

6We have sinned, as did also our fathers; we have committed iniquity, we have done wickedly.

7Our fathers in Egypt understood not nor appreciated Your miracles; they did not [earnestly] remember the multitude of Your mercies nor imprint Your loving-kindness [on their hearts], but they were rebellious and provoked the Lord at the sea, even at the Red Sea.

⁸Nevertheless He saved them for His name's sake [to prove the righteousness of the divine character], that He might make His mighty power known.

⁹He rebuked the Red Sea also, and it dried up; so He led them through the depths as through a pastureland.

¹⁰And He saved them from the hand of him that hated them, and redeemed them from the hand of the [Egyptian] enemy.

¹¹And the waters covered their adversaries; not one of them was left.

¹²Then [Israel] believed His words [trusting in, relying on them]; they sang His praise.

¹³But they hastily forgot His works; they did not [earnestly] wait for His plans regarding them,

¹⁴But lusted exceedingly in the wilderness and tempted and tried to restrain God [with their insistent desires] in the desert.

¹⁵And He gave them their request, but sent leanness into their souls and [thinned their numbers by] disease and death.

¹⁶They envied Moses also in the camp, and Aaron [the high priest], the holy one of the Lord.

¹⁷Therefore the earth opened and swallowed up Dathan and closed over the company of Abiram.

¹⁸And a fire broke out in their company; the flame burned up the wicked.

¹⁹They made a calf in Horeb and worshiped a molten image.

²⁰Thus they exchanged Him Who was their Glory for the image of an ox that eats grass [they traded their Honor for the image of a calf]!

²¹They forgot God their Savior, Who had done such great things in Egypt,

²²Wonders and miracles in the land of Ham, dreadful and awesome things at the Red Sea.

²³Therefore He said He would destroy them. [And He would have done so] had not Moses, His chosen one, stepped into the breach before Him to turn away His threatening wrath.

²⁴Then they spurned and despised the pleasant and desirable land [Canaan]; they believed not His word [neither trusting in, relying on, nor holding to it];

²⁵But they murmured in their tents and hearkened not to the voice of the Lord.

²⁶Therefore He lifted up His hand [as if taking an oath] against them, that He would cause them to fall in the wilderness,

²⁷Cast out their descendants among the nations, and scatter them in the lands [of the earth].

²⁸They joined themselves also to the [idol] Baal of Peor and ate sacrifices [offered] to the lifeless [gods].

²⁹Thus they provoked the Lord to anger with their practices, and a plague broke out among them.

³⁰Then stood up Phinehas [the priest] and executed judgment, and so the plague was stayed.

³¹And that was credited to him for righteousness (right doing and right standing with God) to all generations forever.

³²They angered the Lord also at the waters of Meribah, so that it went ill with Moses for their sakes;

³³For they provoked [Moses'] spirit, so that he spoke unadvisedly with his lips.

³⁴They did not destroy the [heathen] nations as the Lord commanded them,

³⁵But mingled themselves with the [idolatrous] nations and learned their ways and works

³⁶And served their idols, which were a snare to them.

³⁷Yes, they sacrificed their sons and their daughters to demons

³⁸And shed innocent blood, even the blood of their sons and of their daughters, whom they sacrificed to the idols of Canaan; and the land was polluted with their blood.

³⁹Thus were they defiled by their own works, and they played the harlot and practiced idolatry with their own deeds [of idolatrous rites].

⁴⁰Therefore was the wrath of the Lord kindled against His people, insomuch that He abhorred and rejected His own heritage.

⁴¹And He gave them into the hands of the [heathen] nations, and they that hated them ruled over them.

⁴²Their enemies also oppressed them, and they were brought into subjection under the hand of their foes.

⁴³Many times did [God] deliver them, but they were rebellious in their counsel and sank low through their iniquity.

⁴⁴Nevertheless He regarded their distress when He heard their cry;

[45]And He [earnestly] remembered for their sake His covenant and relented their sentence of evil [comforting and easing Himself] according to the abundance of His mercy and loving-kindness [when they cried out to Him].

[46]He also caused [Israel] to find sympathy among those who had carried them away captive.

[47]Deliver us, O Lord our God, and gather us from among the nations, that we may give thanks to Your holy name and glory in praising You.

[48]Blessed (affectionately and gratefully praised) be the Lord, the God of Israel, from everlasting to everlasting! And let all the people say, Amen! Praise the Lord! (Hallelujah!)

PSALM 107

[1]O GIVE thanks to the Lord, for He is good; for His mercy and loving-kindness endure forever!

[2]Let the redeemed of the Lord say so, whom He has delivered from the hand of the adversary,

[3]And gathered them out of the lands, from the east and from the west, from the north and from the [Red] Sea in the south.

[4]Some wandered in the wilderness in a solitary desert track; they found no city for habitation.

[5]Hungry and thirsty, they fainted; their lives were near to being extinguished.

[6]Then they cried to the Lord in their trouble, and He delivered them out of their distresses.

[7]He led them forth by the straight and right way, that they might go to a city where they could establish their homes.

[8]Oh, that men would praise [and confess to] the Lord for His goodness and loving-kindness and His wonderful works to the children of men!

[9]For He satisfies the longing soul and fills the hungry soul with good.

[10]Some sat in darkness and in the shadow of death, being bound in affliction and in irons,

[11]Because they had rebelled against the words of God and spurned the counsel of the Most High.

¹²Therefore He bowed down their hearts with hard labor; they stumbled and fell down, and there was none to help.

¹³Then they cried to the Lord in their trouble, and He saved them out of their distresses.

¹⁴He brought them out of darkness and the shadow of death and broke apart the bonds that held them.

¹⁵Oh, that men would praise [and confess to] the Lord for His goodness and loving-kindness and His wonderful works to the children of men!

¹⁶For He has broken the gates of bronze and cut the bars of iron apart.

¹⁷Some are fools [made ill] because of the way of their transgressions and are afflicted because of their iniquities.

¹⁸They loathe every kind of food, and they draw near to the gates of death.

¹⁹Then they cry to the Lord in their trouble, and He delivers them out of their distresses.

²⁰He sends forth His word and heals them and rescues them from the pit and destruction.

²¹Oh, that men would praise [and confess to] the Lord for His goodness and loving-kindness and His wonderful works to the children of men!

²²And let them sacrifice the sacrifices of thanksgiving and rehearse His deeds with shouts of joy and singing!

²³Some go down to the sea and travel over it in ships to do business in great waters;

²⁴These see the works of the Lord and His wonders in the deep.

²⁵For He commands and raises up the stormy wind, which lifts up the waves of the sea.

²⁶[Those aboard] mount up to the heavens, they go down again to the deeps; their courage melts away because of their plight.

²⁷They reel to and fro and stagger like a drunken man and are at their wits' end [all their wisdom has come to nothing].

²⁸Then they cry to the Lord in their trouble, and He brings them out of their distresses.

²⁹He hushes the storm to a calm and to a gentle whisper, so that the waves of the sea are still.

³⁰Then the men are glad because of the calm, and He brings them to their desired haven.

[31]Oh, that men would praise [and confess to] the Lord for His goodness and loving-kindness and His wonderful works to the children of men!

[32]Let them exalt Him also in the congregation of the people and praise Him in the company of the elders.

[33]He turns rivers into a wilderness, water springs into a thirsty ground,

[34]A fruitful land into a barren, salt waste, because of the wickedness of those who dwell in it.

[35]He turns a wilderness into a pool of water and a dry ground into water springs;

[36]And there He makes the hungry to dwell, that they may prepare a city for habitation,

[37]And sow fields, and plant vineyards which yield fruits of increase.

[38]He blesses them also, so that they are multiplied greatly, and allows not their cattle to decrease.

[39]When they are diminished and bowed down through oppression, trouble, and sorrow,

[40]He pours contempt upon princes and causes them to wander in waste places where there is no road.

[41]Yet He raises the poor and needy from affliction and makes their families like a flock.

[42]The upright shall see it and be glad, but all iniquity shall shut its mouth.

[43]Whoso is wise [if there be any truly wise] will observe and heed these things; and they will diligently consider the mercy and loving-kindness of the Lord.

PSALM 108

A song. A Psalm of David.

[1]O GOD, my heart is fixed (steadfast, in the confidence of faith); I will sing, yes, I will sing praises, even with my glory [all the faculties and powers of one created in Your image]!

[2]Awake, harp and lyre; I myself will wake very early--I will waken the dawn!

[3]I will praise and give thanks to You, O Lord, among the peoples; and I will sing praises unto You among the nations.

⁴For Your mercy and loving-kindness are great and high as the heavens! Your truth and faithfulness reach to the skies!

⁵Be exalted, O God, above the heavens, and let Your glory be over all the earth.

⁶That Your beloved [followers] may be delivered, save with Your right hand and answer us! [or me]!

⁷God has promised in His holiness [regarding the establishment of David's dynasty]: I will rejoice, I will distribute [Canaan among My people], dividing Shechem and [the western region and allotting the eastern region which contains] the Valley of Succoth.

⁸Gilead is Mine, Manasseh is Mine; Ephraim also is My stronghold and the defense of My head; Judah is My scepter and lawgiver.

⁹Moab is My washbasin; upon Edom [My slave] My shoe I cast [to be cleaned]; over Philistia I shout [in triumph].

¹⁰Who will bring me [David] into the strong, fortified city [of Petra]? Who will lead me into Edom?

¹¹Have You not cast us off, O God? And will You not go forth, O God, with our armies?

¹²Give us help against the adversary, for vain is the help of man.

¹³Through and with God we shall do valiantly, for He it is Who shall tread down our adversaries.

PSALM 109

To the Chief Musician. A Psalm of David.

¹O GOD of my praise! Keep not silence,

²For the mouths of the wicked and the mouth of deceit are opened against me; they have spoken to me and against me with lying tongues.

³They have compassed me about also with words of hatred and have fought against me without a cause.

⁴In return for my love they are my adversaries, but I resort to prayer.

⁵And they have rewarded and laid upon me evil for good, and hatred for my love.

⁶Set a wicked man over him [as a judge], and let [a malicious] accuser stand at his right hand.

⁷When [the wicked] is judged, let him be condemned, and let his prayer [for leniency] be turned into a sin.

⁸Let his days be few; and let another take his office and charge.

⁹Let his children be fatherless and his wife a widow.

¹⁰Let his children be continual vagabonds [as was Cain] and beg; let them seek their bread and be driven far from their ruined homes.

¹¹Let the creditor and extortioner seize all that he has; and let strangers (barbarians and foreigners) plunder the fruits of his labor.

¹²Let there be none to extend or continue mercy and kindness to him, neither let there be any to have pity on his fatherless children.

¹³Let his posterity be cut off, and in the generation following let their names be blotted out.

¹⁴Let the iniquity of his fathers be remembered by the Lord; and let not the sin of his mother be blotted out.

¹⁵Let them be before the Lord continually, that He may cut off the memory of them from the earth!--

¹⁶Because the man did not [earnestly] remember to show mercy, but pursued and persecuted the poor and needy man, and the broken in heart [he was ready] to slay.

¹⁷Yes, he loved cursing, and it came [back] upon him; he delighted not in blessing, and it was far from him.

¹⁸He clothed himself also with cursing as with his garment, and it seeped into his inward [life] like water, and like oil into his bones.

¹⁹Let it be to him as the raiment with which he covers himself and as the girdle with which he is girded continually.

²⁰Let this be the reward of my adversaries from the Lord, and of those who speak evil against my life.

²¹But You deal with me and act for me, O God the Lord, for Your name's sake; because Your mercy and loving-kindness are good, O deliver me.

²²For I am poor and needy, and my heart is wounded and stricken within me.

²³I am gone like the shadow when it lengthens and declines; I toss up and down and am shaken off as the locust.

²⁴My knees are weak and totter from fasting; and my body is gaunt and has no fatness.

²⁵I have become also a reproach and a taunt to others; when they see me, they shake their heads.

²⁶Help me, O Lord my God; O save me according to Your mercy and loving-kindness!--

²⁷That they may know that this is Your hand, that You, Lord, have done it.

²⁸Let them curse, but do You bless. When adversaries arise, let them be put to shame, but let Your servant rejoice.

²⁹Let my adversaries be clothed with shame and dishonor, and let them cover themselves with their own disgrace and confusion as with a robe.

³⁰I will give great praise and thanks to the Lord with my mouth; yes, and I will praise Him among the multitude.

³¹For He will stand at the right hand of the poor and needy, to save him from those who condemn his life.

PSALM 110

A Psalm of David.

¹THE LORD (God) says to my Lord (the Messiah), Sit at My right hand, until I make Your adversaries Your footstool.

²The Lord will send forth from Zion the scepter of Your strength; rule, then, in the midst of Your foes.

³Your people will offer themselves willingly in the day of Your power, in the beauty of holiness and in holy array out of the womb of the morning; to You [will spring forth] Your young men, who are as the dew.

⁴The Lord has sworn and will not revoke or change it: You are a priest forever, after the manner and order of Melchizedek.

⁵The Lord at Your right hand will shatter kings in the day of His indignation.

⁶He will execute judgment [in overwhelming punishment] upon the nations; He will fill the valleys with the dead bodies, He will crush the [chief] heads over lands many and far extended.

⁷He will drink of the brook by the way; therefore will He lift up His head [triumphantly].

PSALM 111

¹PRAISE THE Lord! (Hallelujah!) I will praise and give thanks to the Lord with my whole heart in the council of the upright and in the congregation.

²The works of the Lord are great, sought out by all those who have delight in them.

³His work is honorable and glorious, and His righteousness endures forever.

⁴He has made His wonderful works to be remembered; the Lord is gracious, merciful, and full of loving compassion.

⁵He has given food and provision to those who reverently and worshipfully fear Him; He will remember His covenant forever and imprint it [on His mind].

⁶He has declared and shown to His people the power of His works in giving them the heritage of the nations [of Canaan].

⁷The works of His hands are [absolute] truth and justice [faithful and right]; and all His decrees and precepts are sure (fixed, established, and trustworthy).

⁸They stand fast and are established forever and ever and are done in [absolute] truth and uprightness.

⁹He has sent redemption to His people; He has commanded His covenant to be forever; holy is His name, inspiring awe, reverence, and godly fear.

¹⁰The reverent fear and worship of the Lord is the beginning of Wisdom and skill [the preceding and the first essential, the prerequisite and the alphabet]; a good understanding, wisdom, and meaning have all those who do [the will of the Lord]. Their praise of Him endures forever.

PSALM 112

¹PRAISE THE Lord! (Hallelujah!) Blessed (happy, fortunate, to be envied) is the man who fears (reveres and worships) the Lord, who delights greatly in His commandments.

²His [spiritual] offspring shall be mighty upon earth; the generation of the upright shall be blessed.

³Prosperity and welfare are in his house, and his righteousness endures forever.

⁴Light arises in the darkness for the upright, gracious, compassionate, and just [who are in right standing with God].

⁵It is well with the man who deals generously and lends, who conducts his affairs with justice.

⁶He will not be moved forever; the [uncompromisingly] righteous (the upright, in right standing with God) shall be in everlasting remembrance.

⁷He shall not be afraid of evil tidings; his heart is firmly fixed, trusting (leaning on and being confident) in the Lord.

⁸His heart is established and steady, he will not be afraid while he waits to see his desire established upon his adversaries.

⁹He has distributed freely [he has given to the poor and needy]; his righteousness (uprightness and right standing with God) endures forever; his horn shall be exalted in honor.

¹⁰The wicked man will see it and be grieved and angered, he will gnash his teeth and disappear [in despair]; the desire of the wicked shall perish and come to nothing.

PSALM 113

¹PRAISE THE Lord! (Hallelujah!) Praise, O servants of the Lord, praise the name of the Lord!

²Blessed be the name of the Lord from this time forth and forever

³From the rising of the sun to the going down of it and from east to west, the name of the Lord is to be praised!

⁴The Lord is high above all nations, and His glory above the heavens!

⁵Who is like the Lord our God, Who has His seat on high,

⁶Who humbles Himself to regard the heavens and the earth!

⁷[The Lord] raises the poor out of the dust and lifts the needy from the ash heap and the dung hill,

⁸That He may seat them with princes, even with the princes of His people.

⁹He makes the barren woman to be a homemaker and a joyful mother of [spiritual] children. Praise the Lord! (Hallelujah!)

PSALM 114

¹WHEN ISRAEL came forth out of Egypt, the house of Jacob from a people of strange language,

²Judah became [God's] sanctuary (the Holy Place of His habitation), and Israel His dominion.

³The [Red] Sea looked and fled; the Jordan [River] was turned back.

⁴The mountains skipped like rams, the little hills like lambs.

⁵What ails you, O [Red] Sea, that you flee? O Jordan, that you turn back?

⁶You mountains, that you skip like rams, and you little hills, like lambs?

⁷Tremble, O earth, at the presence of the Lord, at the presence of the God of Jacob,

⁸Who turned the rock into a pool of water, the flint into a fountain of waters.

PSALM 115

¹NOT TO us, O Lord, not to us but to Your name give glory, for Your mercy and loving-kindness and for the sake of Your truth and faithfulness!

²Why should the nations say, Where is now their God?

³But our God is in heaven; He does whatever He pleases.

⁴The idols of the nations are silver and gold, the work of men's hands.

⁵They have mouths, but they speak not; eyes have they, but they see not;

⁶They have ears, but they hear not; noses have they, but they smell not;

⁷They have hands, but they handle not; feet have they, but they walk not; neither can they make a sound with their throats.

⁸They who make idols are like them; so are all who trust in and lean on them.

⁹O Israel, trust and take refuge in the Lord! [Lean on, rely on, and be confident in Him!] He is their Help and their Shield.

¹⁰O house of Aaron [the priesthood], trust in and lean on the Lord! He is their Help and their Shield.

¹¹You who [reverently] fear the Lord, trust in and lean on the Lord! He is their Help and their Shield.

¹²The Lord has been mindful of us, He will bless us: He will bless the house of Israel, He will bless the house of Aaron [the priesthood],

¹³He will bless those who reverently and worshipfully fear the Lord, both small and great.

¹⁴May the Lord give you increase more and more, you and your children.

¹⁵May you be blessed of the Lord, Who made heaven and earth!

¹⁶The heavens are the Lord's heavens, but the earth has He given to the children of men.

¹⁷The dead praise not the Lord, neither any who go down into silence.

¹⁸But we will bless (affectionately and gratefully praise) the Lord from this time forth and forever. Praise the Lord! (Hallelujah!)

PSALM 116

¹I LOVE the Lord, because He has heard [and now hears] my voice and my supplications.

²Because He has inclined His ear to me, therefore will I call upon Him as long as I live.

³The cords and sorrows of death were around me, and the terrors of Sheol (the place of the dead) had laid hold of me; I suffered anguish and grief (trouble and sorrow).

⁴Then called I upon the name of the Lord: O Lord, I beseech You, save my life and deliver me!

⁵Gracious is the Lord, and [rigidly] righteous; yes, our God is merciful.

⁶The Lord preserves the simple; I was brought low, and He helped and saved me.

⁷Return to your rest, O my soul, for the Lord has dealt bountifully with you.

⁸For You have delivered my life from death, my eyes from tears, and my feet from stumbling and falling.

⁹I will walk before the Lord in the land of the living.

¹⁰I believed (trusted in, relied on, and clung to my God), and therefore have I spoken [even when I said], I am greatly afflicted.

¹¹I said in my haste, All men are deceitful and liars.

¹²What shall I render to the Lord for all His benefits toward me? [How can I repay Him for all His bountiful dealings?]

¹³I will lift up the cup of salvation and deliverance and call on the name of the Lord.

¹⁴I will pay my vows to the Lord, yes, in the presence of all His people.

¹⁵Precious (important and no light matter) in the sight of the Lord is the death of His saints (His loving ones).

¹⁶O Lord, truly I am Your servant; I am Your servant, the son of Your handmaid; You have loosed my bonds.

¹⁷I will offer to You the sacrifice of thanksgiving and will call on the name of the Lord.

¹⁸I will pay my vows to the Lord, yes, in the presence of all His people,

¹⁹In the courts of the Lord's house--in the midst of you, O Jerusalem. Praise the Lord! (Hallelujah!)

PSALM 117

¹O PRAISE the Lord, all you nations! Praise Him, all you people!

²For His mercy and loving-kindness are great toward us, and the truth and faithfulness of the Lord endure forever. Praise the Lord! (Hallelujah!)

PSALM 118

¹O GIVE thanks to the Lord, for He is good; for His mercy and loving-kindness endure forever!

²Let Israel now say that His mercy and loving-kindness endure forever.

³Let the house of Aaron [the priesthood] now say that His mercy and loving-kindness endure forever.

⁴Let those now who reverently and worshipfully fear the Lord say that His mercy and loving-kindness endure forever.

⁵Out of my distress I called upon the Lord; the Lord answered me and set me free and in a large place.

⁶The Lord is on my side; I will not fear. What can man do to me?

⁷The Lord is on my side and takes my part, He is among those who help me; therefore shall I see my desire established upon those who hate me.

⁸It is better to trust and take refuge in the Lord than to put confidence in man.

⁹It is better to trust and take refuge in the Lord than to put confidence in princes.

¹⁰All nations (the surrounding tribes) compassed me about, but in the name of the Lord I will cut them off!

¹¹They compassed me about, yes, they surrounded me on every side; but in the name of the Lord I will cut them off!

¹²They swarmed about me like bees, they blaze up and are extinguished like a fire of thorns; in the name of the Lord I will cut them off!

¹³You [my adversary] thrust sorely at me that I might fall, but the Lord helped me.

¹⁴The Lord is my Strength and Song; and He has become my Salvation.

¹⁵The voice of rejoicing and salvation is in the tents and private dwellings of the [uncompromisingly] righteous: the right hand of the Lord does valiantly and achieves strength!

¹⁶The right hand of the Lord is exalted; the right hand of the Lord does valiantly and achieves strength!

¹⁷I shall not die but live, and shall declare the works and recount the illustrious acts of the Lord.

¹⁸The Lord has chastened me sorely, but He has not given me over to death.

¹⁹Open to me the [temple] gates of righteousness; I will enter through them, and I will confess and praise the Lord.

²⁰This is the gate of the Lord; the [uncompromisingly] righteous shall enter through it.

²¹I will confess, praise, and give thanks to You, for You have heard and answered me; and You have become my Salvation and Deliverer.

²²The stone which the builders rejected has become the chief cornerstone.

²³This is from the Lord and is His doing; it is marvelous in our eyes.

²⁴This is the day which the Lord has brought about; we will rejoice and be glad in it.

²⁵Save now, we beseech You, O Lord; send now prosperity, O Lord, we beseech You, and give to us success!

²⁶Blessed is he who comes in the name of the Lord; we bless you from the house of the Lord [you who come into His sanctuary under His guardianship].

[27]The Lord is God, Who has shown and given us light [He has illuminated us with grace, freedom, and joy]. Decorate the festival with leafy boughs and bind the sacrifices to be offered with thick cords [all over the priest's court, right up] to the horns of the altar.

[28]You are my God, and I will confess, praise, and give thanks to You; You are my God, I will extol You.

[29]O give thanks to the Lord, for He is good; for His mercy and loving-kindness endure forever.

PSALM 119

[1]BLESSED (HAPPY, fortunate, to be envied) are the undefiled (the upright, truly sincere, and blameless) in the way [of the revealed will of God], who walk (order their conduct and conversation) in the law of the Lord (the whole of God's revealed will).

[2]Blessed (happy, fortunate, to be envied) are they who keep His testimonies, and who seek, inquire for and of Him and crave Him with the whole heart.

[3]Yes, they do no unrighteousness [no willful wandering from His precepts]; they walk in His ways.

[4]You have commanded us to keep Your precepts, that we should observe them diligently.

[5]Oh, that my ways were directed and established to observe Your statutes [hearing, receiving, loving, and obeying them]!

[6]Then shall I not be put to shame [by failing to inherit Your promises] when I have respect to all Your commandments.

[7]I will praise and give thanks to You with uprightness of heart when I learn [by sanctified experiences] Your righteous judgments [Your decisions against and punishments for particular lines of thought and conduct].

[8]I will keep Your statutes; O forsake me not utterly.

[9]How shall a young man cleanse his way? By taking heed and keeping watch [on himself] according to Your word [conforming his life to it].

[10]With my whole heart have I sought You, inquiring for and of You and yearning for You; Oh, let me not wander or step aside [either in ignorance or willfully] from Your commandments.

[11]Your word have I laid up in my heart, that I might not sin against You.

¹²Blessed are You, O Lord; teach me Your statutes.

¹³With my lips have I declared and recounted all the ordinances of Your mouth.

¹⁴I have rejoiced in the way of Your testimonies as much as in all riches.

¹⁵I will meditate on Your precepts and have respect to Your ways [the paths of life marked out by Your law].

¹⁶I will delight myself in Your statutes; I will not forget Your word.

¹⁷Deal bountifully with Your servant, that I may live; and I will observe Your word [hearing, receiving, loving, and obeying it].

¹⁸Open my eyes, that I may behold wondrous things out of Your law.

¹⁹I am a stranger and a temporary resident on the earth; hide not Your commandments from me.

²⁰My heart is breaking with the longing that it has for Your ordinances and judgments at all times.

²¹You rebuke the proud and arrogant, the accursed ones, who err and wander from Your commandments.

²²Take away from me reproach and contempt, for I keep Your testimonies.

²³Princes also sat and talked against me, but Your servant meditated on Your statutes.

²⁴Your testimonies also are my delight and my counselors.

²⁵My earthly life cleaves to the dust; revive and stimulate me according to Your word!

²⁶I have declared my ways and opened my griefs to You, and You listened to me; teach me Your statutes.

²⁷Make me understand the way of Your precepts; so shall I meditate on and talk of Your wondrous works.

²⁸My life dissolves and weeps itself away for heaviness; raise me up and strengthen me according to [the promises of] Your word.

²⁹Remove from me the way of falsehood and unfaithfulness [to You], and graciously impart Your law to me.

³⁰I have chosen the way of truth and faithfulness; Your ordinances have I set before me.

³¹I cleave to Your testimonies; O Lord, put me not to shame!

³²I will [not merely walk, but] run the way of Your commandments, when You give me a heart that is willing.

³³Teach me, O Lord, the way of Your statutes, and I will keep it to the end [steadfastly].

³⁴Give me understanding, that I may keep Your law; yes, I will observe it with my whole heart.

³⁵Make me go in the path of Your commandments, for in them do I delight.

³⁶Incline my heart to Your testimonies and not to covetousness (robbery, sensuality, unworthy riches).

³⁷Turn away my eyes from beholding vanity (idols and idolatry); and restore me to vigorous life and health in Your ways.

³⁸Establish Your word and confirm Your promise to Your servant, which is for those who reverently fear and devotedly worship You.

³⁹Turn away my reproach which I fear and dread, for Your ordinances are good.

⁴⁰Behold, I long for Your precepts; in Your righteousness give me renewed life.

⁴¹Let Your mercy and loving-kindness come also to me, O Lord, even Your salvation according to Your promise;

⁴²Then shall I have an answer for those who taunt and reproach me, for I lean on, rely on, and trust in Your word.

⁴³And take not the word of truth utterly out of my mouth, for I hope in Your ordinances.

⁴⁴I will keep Your law continually, forever and ever [hearing, receiving, loving, and obeying it].

⁴⁵And I will walk at liberty and at ease, for I have sought and inquired for [and desperately required] Your precepts.

⁴⁶I will speak of Your testimonies also before kings and will not be put to shame.

⁴⁷For I will delight myself in Your commandments, which I love.

⁴⁸My hands also will I lift up [in fervent supplication] to Your commandments, which I love, and I will meditate on Your statutes.

⁴⁹Remember [fervently] the word and promise to Your servant, in which You have caused me to hope.

⁵⁰This is my comfort and consolation in my affliction: that Your word has revived me and given me life.

⁵¹The proud have had me greatly in derision, yet have I not declined in my interest in or turned aside from Your law.

⁵²When I have [earnestly] recalled Your ordinances from of old, O Lord, I have taken comfort.

⁵³Burning indignation, terror, and sadness seize upon me because of the wicked, who forsake Your law.

⁵⁴Your statutes have been my songs in the house of my pilgrimage.

⁵⁵I have [earnestly] remembered Your name, O Lord, in the night, and I have observed Your law.

⁵⁶This I have had [as the gift of Your grace and as my reward]: that I have kept Your precepts [hearing, receiving, loving, and obeying them].

⁵⁷You are my portion, O Lord; I have promised to keep Your words.

⁵⁸I entreated Your favor with my whole heart; be merciful and gracious to me according to Your promise.

⁵⁹I considered my ways; I turned my feet to [obey] Your testimonies.

⁶⁰I made haste and delayed not to keep Your commandments.

⁶¹Though the cords of the wicked have enclosed and ensnared me, I have not forgotten Your law.

⁶²At midnight I will rise to give thanks to You because of Your righteous ordinances.

⁶³I am a companion of all those who fear, revere, and worship You, and of those who observe and give heed to Your precepts.

⁶⁴The earth, O Lord, is full of Your mercy and loving-kindness; teach me Your statutes.

⁶⁵You have dealt well with Your servant, O Lord, according to Your promise.

⁶⁶Teach me good judgment, wise and right discernment, and knowledge, for I have believed (trusted, relied on, and clung to) Your commandments.

⁶⁷Before I was afflicted I went astray, but now Your word do I keep [hearing, receiving, loving, and obeying it].

⁶⁸You are good and kind and do good; teach me Your statutes.

⁶⁹The arrogant and godless have put together a lie against me, but I will keep Your precepts with my whole heart.

⁷⁰Their hearts are as fat as grease [their minds are dull and brutal], but I delight in Your law.

⁷¹It is good for me that I have been afflicted, that I might learn Your statutes.

⁷²The law from Your mouth is better to me than thousands of gold and silver pieces.

⁷³Your hands have made me, cunningly fashioned and established me; give me understanding, that I may learn Your commandments.

⁷⁴Those who reverently and worshipfully fear You will see me and be glad, because I have hoped in Your word and tarried for it.

⁷⁵I know, O Lord, that Your judgments are right and righteous, and that in faithfulness You have afflicted me.

⁷⁶Let, I pray You, Your merciful kindness and steadfast love be for my comfort, according to Your promise to Your servant.

⁷⁷Let Your tender mercy and loving-kindness come to me that I may live, for Your law is my delight!

⁷⁸Let the proud be put to shame, for they dealt perversely with me without a cause; but I will meditate on Your precepts.

⁷⁹Let those who reverently and worshipfully fear You turn to me, and those who have known Your testimonies.

⁸⁰Let my heart be sound (sincere and wholehearted and blameless) in Your statutes, that I may not be put to shame.

⁸¹My soul languishes and grows faint for Your salvation, but I hope in Your word.

⁸²My eyes fail, watching for [the fulfillment of] Your promise. I say, When will You comfort me?

⁸³For I have become like a bottle [a wineskin blackened and shriveled] in the smoke [in which it hangs], yet do I not forget Your statutes.

⁸⁴How many are the days of Your servant? When will You judge those who pursue and persecute me?

⁸⁵The godless and arrogant have dug pitfalls for me, men who do not conform to Your law.

⁸⁶All Your commandments are faithful and sure. [The godless] pursue and persecute me with falsehood; help me [Lord]!

⁸⁷They had almost consumed me upon earth, but I forsook not Your precepts.

⁸⁸According to Your steadfast love give life to me; then I will keep the testimony of Your mouth [hearing, receiving, loving, and obeying it].

⁸⁹Forever, O Lord, Your word is settled in heaven [stands firm as the heavens].

⁹⁰Your faithfulness is from generation to generation; You have established the earth, and it stands fast.

⁹¹All [the whole universe] are Your servants; therefore they continue this day according to Your ordinances.

⁹²Unless Your law had been my delight, I would have perished in my affliction.

⁹³I will never forget Your precepts, [how can I?] for it is by them You have quickened me (granted me life).

⁹⁴I am Yours, therefore save me [Your own]; for I have sought (inquired of and for) Your precepts and required them [as my urgent need].

⁹⁵The wicked wait for me to destroy me, but I will consider Your testimonies.

⁹⁶I have seen that everything [human] has its limits and end [no matter how extensive, noble, and excellent]; but Your commandment is exceedingly broad and extends without limits [into eternity].

⁹⁷Oh, how love I Your law! It is my meditation all the day.

⁹⁸You, through Your commandments, make me wiser than my enemies, for Your words are ever before me.

⁹⁹I have better understanding and deeper insight than all my teachers, because Your testimonies are my meditation.

¹⁰⁰I understand more than the aged, because I keep Your precepts [hearing, receiving, loving, and obeying them].

¹⁰¹I have restrained my feet from every evil way, that I might keep Your word [hearing, receiving, loving, and obeying it].

¹⁰²I have not turned aside from Your ordinances, for You Yourself have taught me.

¹⁰³How sweet are Your words to my taste, sweeter than honey to my mouth!

¹⁰⁴Through Your precepts I get understanding; therefore I hate every false way.

¹⁰⁵Your word is a lamp to my feet and a light to my path.

¹⁰⁶I have sworn [an oath] and have confirmed it, that I will keep Your righteous ordinances [hearing, receiving, loving, and obeying them].

¹⁰⁷I am sorely afflicted; renew and quicken me [give me life], O Lord, according to Your word!

¹⁰⁸Accept, I beseech You, the freewill offerings of my mouth, O Lord, and teach me Your ordinances.

[109]My life is continually in my hand, yet I do not forget Your law.

[110]The wicked have laid a snare for me, yet I do not stray from Your precepts.

[111]Your testimonies have I taken as a heritage forever, for they are the rejoicing of my heart.

[112]I have inclined my heart to perform Your statutes forever, even to the end.

[113]I hate the thoughts of undecided [in religion], double-minded people, but Your law do I love.

[114]You are my hiding place and my shield; I hope in Your word.

[115]Depart from me, you evildoers, that I may keep the commandments of my God [hearing, receiving, loving, and obeying them].

[116]Uphold me according to Your promise, that I may live; and let me not be put to shame in my hope!

[117]Hold me up, that I may be safe and have regard for Your statutes continually!

[118]You spurn and set at nought all those who stray from Your statutes, for their own lying deceives them and their tricks are in vain.

[119]You put away and count as dross all the wicked of the earth [for there is no true metal in them]; therefore I love Your testimonies.

[120]My flesh trembles and shudders for fear and reverential, worshipful awe of You, and I am afraid and in dread of Your judgments.

[121]I have done justice and righteousness; leave me not to those who would oppress me.

[122]Be surety for Your servant for good [as Judah was surety for the safety of Benjamin]; let not the proud oppress me.

[123]My eyes fail, watching for Your salvation and for the fulfillment of Your righteous promise.

[124]Deal with Your servant according to Your mercy and loving-kindness, and teach me Your statutes.

[125]I am Your servant; give me understanding (discernment and comprehension), that I may know (discern and be familiar with the character of) Your testimonies.

[126]It is time for the Lord to act; they have frustrated Your law.

[127]Therefore I love Your commandments more than [resplendent] gold, yes, more than refined gold.

128Therefore I esteem as right all, yes, all Your precepts; I hate every false way.

129Your testimonies are wonderful [far exceeding anything conceived by man]; therefore my [penitent] self keeps them [hearing, receiving, loving, and obeying them].

130The entrance and unfolding of Your words give light; their unfolding gives understanding (discernment and comprehension) to the simple.

131I opened my mouth and panted [with eager desire], for I longed for Your commandments.

132Look upon me, be merciful unto me, and show me favor, as is Your way to those who love Your name.

133Establish my steps and direct them by [means of] Your word; let not any iniquity have dominion over me.

134Deliver me from the oppression of man; so will I keep Your precepts [hearing, receiving, loving, and obeying them].

135Make Your face shine [with pleasure] upon Your servant, and teach me Your statutes.

136Streams of water run down my eyes, because men do not keep Your law [they hear it not, nor receive it, love it, or obey it].

137[Rigidly] righteous are You, O Lord, and upright are Your judgments and all expressions of Your will.

138You have commanded and appointed Your testimonies in righteousness and in great faithfulness.

139My zeal has consumed me and cut me off, because my adversaries have forgotten Your words.

140Your word is very pure (tried and well refined); therefore Your servant loves it.

141I am small (insignificant) and despised, but I do not forget Your precepts.

142Your righteousness is an everlasting righteousness, and Your law is truth.

143Trouble and anguish have found and taken hold on me, yet Your commandments are my delight.

144Your righteous testimonies are everlasting and Your decrees are binding to eternity; give me understanding and I shall live [give me discernment and comprehension and I shall not die].

[145]I cried with my whole heart; hear me, O Lord; I will keep Your statutes [I will hear, receive, love, and obey them].

[146]I cried to You; save me, that I may keep Your testimonies [hearing, receiving, loving, and obeying them].

[147]I anticipated the dawning of the morning and cried [in childlike prayer]; I hoped in Your word.

[148]My eyes anticipate the night watches and I am awake before the cry of the watchman, that I may meditate on Your word.

[149]Hear my voice according to Your steadfast love; O Lord, quicken me and give me life according to Your [righteous] decrees.

[150]They draw near who follow after wrong thinking and persecute me with wickedness; they are far from Your law.

[151]You are near, O Lord [nearer to me than my foes], and all Your commandments are truth.

[152]Of old have I known Your testimonies, and for a long time, [therefore it is a thoroughly established conviction] that You have founded them forever.

[153]Consider my affliction and deliver me, for I do not forget Your law.

[154]Plead my cause and redeem me; revive me and give me life according to Your word.

[155]Salvation is far from the wicked, for they seek not nor hunger for Your statutes.

[156]Great are Your tender mercy and loving-kindness, O Lord; give me life according to Your ordinances.

[157]Many are my persecutors and my adversaries, yet I do not swerve from Your testimonies.

[158]I behold the treacherous and am grieved and loathe them, because they do not respect Your law [neither hearing, receiving, loving, nor obeying it].

[159]Consider how I love Your precepts; revive me and give life to me, O Lord, according to Your loving-kindness!

[160]The sum of Your word is truth [the total of the full meaning of all Your individual precepts]; and every one of Your righteous decrees endures forever.

[161]Princes pursue and persecute me without cause, but my heart stands in awe of Your words [dreading violation of them far more than the force of a prince.

[162]I rejoice at Your word as one who finds great spoil.

[163]I hate and abhor falsehood, but Your law do I love.

[164]Seven times a day and all day long do I praise You because of Your righteous decrees.

[165]Great peace have they who love Your law; nothing shall offend them or make them stumble.

[166]I am hoping and waiting [eagerly] for Your salvation, O Lord, and I do Your commandments.

[167]Your testimonies have I kept [hearing, receiving, loving, and obeying them]; I love them exceedingly!

[168]I have observed Your precepts and Your testimonies, for all my ways are [fully known] before You.

[169]Let my mournful cry and supplication come [near] before You, O Lord; give me understanding (discernment and comprehension) according to Your word [of assurance and promise].

[170]Let my supplication come before You; deliver me according to Your word!

[171]My lips shall pour forth praise [with thanksgiving and renewed trust] when You teach me Your statutes.

[172]My tongue shall sing [praise for the fulfillment] of Your word, for all Your commandments are righteous.

[173]Let Your hand be ready to help me, for I have chosen Your precepts.

[174]I have longed for Your salvation, O Lord, and Your law is my delight.

[175]Let me live that I may praise You, and let Your decrees help me.

[176]I have gone astray like a lost sheep; seek, inquire for, and demand Your servant, for I do not forget Your commandments.

PSALM 120

A Song of Ascents.

[1]IN MY distress I cried to the Lord, and He answered me.

[2]Deliver me, O Lord, from lying lips and from deceitful tongues.

[3]What shall be given to you? Or what more shall be done to you, you deceitful tongue?--

[4]Sharp arrows of a [mighty] warrior, with [glowing] coals of the broom tree!

5Woe is me that I sojourn with Meshech, that I dwell beside the tents of Kedar [as if among notoriously barbarous people]!

6My life has too long had its dwelling with him who hates peace.

7I am for peace; but when I speak, they are for war.

PSALM 121
A Song of Ascents.

1I WILL lift up my eyes to the hills [around Jerusalem, to sacred Mount Zion and Mount Moriah]--From whence shall my help come?

2My help comes from the Lord, Who made heaven and earth.

3He will not allow your foot to slip or to be moved; He Who keeps you will not slumber.

4Behold, He who keeps Israel will neither slumber nor sleep.

5The Lord is your keeper; the Lord is your shade on your right hand [the side not carrying a shield].

6The sun shall not smite you by day, nor the moon by night.

7The Lord will keep you from all evil; He will keep your life.

8The Lord will keep your going out and your coming in from this time forth and forevermore.

PSALM 122
A Song of Ascents. Of David.

1I WAS glad when they said to me, Let us go to the house of the Lord!

2Our feet are standing within your gates, O Jerusalem!--

3Jerusalem, which is built as a city that is compacted together--

4To which the tribes go up, even the tribes of the Lord, as was decreed and as a testimony for Israel, to give thanks to the name of the Lord.

5For there the thrones of judgment were set, the thrones of the house of David.

6Pray for the peace of Jerusalem! May they prosper who love you [the Holy City]!

7May peace be within your walls and prosperity within your palaces!

⁸For my brethren and companions' sake, I will now say, Peace be within you!

⁹For the sake of the house of the Lord our God, I will seek, inquire for, and require your good.

PSALM 123
A Song of Ascents.

¹UNTO YOU do I lift up my eyes, O You Who are enthroned in heaven.

²Behold, as the eyes of servants look to the hand of their master, and as the eyes of a maid to the hand of her mistress, so our eyes look to the Lord our God, until He has mercy and loving-kindness for us.

³Have mercy on us, O Lord, have mercy on and loving-kindness for us, for we are exceedingly satiated with contempt.

⁴Our life is exceedingly filled with the scorning and scoffing of those who are at ease and with the contempt of the proud (irresponsible tyrants who disregard God's law).

PSALM 124
A Song of Ascents. Of David.

¹IF IT had not been the Lord Who was on our side--now may Israel say--

²If it had not been the Lord Who was on our side when men rose up against us,

³Then they would have quickly swallowed us up alive when their wrath was kindled against us;

⁴Then the waters would have overwhelmed us and swept us away, the torrent would have gone over us;

⁵Then the proud waters would have gone over us.

⁶Blessed be the Lord, Who has not given us as prey to their teeth!

⁷We are like a bird escaped from the snare of the fowlers; the snare is broken, and we have escaped!

⁸Our help is in the name of the Lord, Who made heaven and earth.

PSALM 125
A Song of Ascents.

[1]THOSE WHO trust in, lean on, and confidently hope in the Lord are like Mount Zion, which cannot be moved but abides and stands fast forever.

[2]As the mountains are round about Jerusalem, so the Lord is round about His people from this time forth and forever.

[3]For the scepter of wickedness shall not rest upon the land of the [uncompromisingly] righteous, lest the righteous (God's people) stretch forth their hands to iniquity and apostasy.

[4]Do good, O Lord, to those who are good, and to those who are right [with You and all people] in their hearts.

[5]As for such as turn aside to their crooked ways [of indifference to God], the Lord will lead them forth with the workers of iniquity. Peace be upon Israel!

PSALM 126
A Song of Ascents.

[1]WHEN THE Lord brought back the captives [who returned] to Zion, we were like those who dream [it seemed so unreal].

[2]Then were our mouths filled with laughter, and our tongues with singing. Then they said among the nations, The Lord has done great things for them.

[3]The Lord has done great things for us! We are glad!

[4]Turn to freedom our captivity and restore our fortunes, O Lord, as the streams in the South (the Negeb) [are restored by the torrents].

[5]They who sow in tears shall reap in joy and singing.

[6]He who goes forth bearing seed and weeping [at needing his precious supply of grain for sowing] shall doubtless come again with rejoicing, bringing his sheaves with him.

PSALM 127
A Song of Ascents. Of Solomon.

[1]EXCEPT THE Lord builds the house, they labor in vain who build it; except the Lord keeps the city, the watchman wakes but in vain.

²It is vain for you to rise up early, to take rest late, to eat the bread of [anxious] toil--for He gives [blessings] to His beloved in sleep.

³Behold, children are a heritage from the Lord, the fruit of the womb a reward.

⁴As arrows are in the hand of a warrior, so are the children of one's youth.

⁵Happy, blessed, and fortunate is the man whose quiver is filled with them! They will not be put to shame when they speak with their adversaries [in gatherings] at the [city's] gate.

PSALM 128

A Song of Ascents.

¹BLESSED (HAPPY, fortunate, to be envied) is everyone who fears, reveres, and worships the Lord, who walks in His ways and lives according to His commandments.

²For you shall eat [the fruit] of the labor of your hands; happy (blessed, fortunate, enviable) shall you be, and it shall be well with you.

³Your wife shall be like a fruitful vine in the innermost parts of your house; your children shall be like olive plants round about your table.

⁴Behold, thus shall the man be blessed who reverently and worshipfully fears the Lord.

⁵May the Lord bless you out of Zion [His sanctuary], and may you see the prosperity of Jerusalem all the days of your life;

⁶Yes, may you see your children's children. Peace be upon Israel!

PSALM 129

A Song of Ascents.

¹MANY A time and much have they afflicted me from my youth up--let Israel now say--

²Many a time and much have they afflicted me from my youth up, yet they have not prevailed against me.

³The plowers plowed upon my back; they made long their furrows.

⁴The Lord is righteous; He has cut asunder the thick cords by which the wicked [enslaved us].

⁵Let them all be put to shame and turned backward who hate Zion.

⁶Let them be as the grass upon the housetops, which withers before it grows up,

⁷With which the mower fills not his hand, nor the binder of sheaves his bosom--

⁸While those who go by do not say, The blessing of the Lord be upon you! We bless you in the name of the Lord!

PSALM 130

A Song of Ascents.

¹OUT OF the depths have I cried to You, O Lord.

²Lord, hear my voice; let Your ears be attentive to the voice of my supplications.

³If You, Lord, should keep account of and treat [us according to our] sins, O Lord, who could stand?

⁴But there is forgiveness with You [just what man needs], that You may be reverently feared and worshiped.

⁵I wait for the Lord, I expectantly wait, and in His word do I hope.

⁶I am looking and waiting for the Lord more than watchmen for the morning, I say, more than watchmen for the morning.

⁷O Israel, hope in the Lord! For with the Lord there is mercy and loving-kindness, and with Him is plenteous redemption.

⁸And He will redeem Israel from all their iniquities.

PSALM 131

A Song of Ascents. Of David.

¹LORD, MY heart is not haughty, nor my eyes lofty; neither do I exercise myself in matters too great or in things too wonderful for me.

²Surely I have calmed and quieted my soul; like a weaned child with his mother, like a weaned child is my soul within me [ceased from fretting].

³O Israel, hope in the Lord from this time forth and forever.

PSALM 132
A Song of Ascents.

¹LORD, [earnestly] remember to David's credit all his humiliations and hardships and endurance--

²How he swore to the Lord and vowed to the Mighty One of Jacob:

³Surely I will not enter my dwelling house or get into my bed--

⁴I will not permit my eyes to sleep or my eyelids to slumber,

⁵Until I have found a place for the Lord, a habitation for the Mighty One of Jacob.

⁶Behold, at Ephratah we [first] heard of [the discovered ark]; we found it in the fields of the wood [at Kiriath-jearim].

⁷Let us go into His tabernacle; let us worship at His footstool.

⁸Arise, O Lord, to Your resting-place, You and the ark [the symbol] of Your strength.

⁹Let Your priests be clothed with righteousness (right living and right standing with God); and let Your saints shout for joy!

¹⁰For Your servant David's sake, turn not away the face of Your anointed and reject not Your own king.

¹¹The Lord swore to David in truth; He will not turn back from it: One of the fruit of your body I will set upon your throne.

¹²If your children will keep My covenant and My testimony that I shall teach them, their children also shall sit upon your throne forever.

¹³For the Lord has chosen Zion, He has desired it for His habitation:

¹⁴This is My resting-place forever [says the Lord]; here will I dwell, for I have desired it.

¹⁵I will surely and abundantly bless her provision; I will satisfy her poor with bread.

¹⁶Her priests also will I clothe with salvation, and her saints shall shout aloud for joy.

¹⁷There will I make a horn spring forth and bud for David; I have ordained and prepared a lamp for My anointed [fulfilling the promises of old].

¹⁸His enemies will I clothe with shame, but upon himself shall his crown flourish.

PSALM 133

A Song of Ascents. Of David.

¹BEHOLD, HOW good and how pleasant it is for brethren to dwell together in unity!

²It is like the precious ointment poured on the head, that ran down on the beard, even the beard of Aaron [the high priest], that came down upon the collar and skirts of his garments [consecrating the whole body].

³It is like the dew of [lofty] Mount Hermon and the dew that comes on the hills of Zion; for there the Lord has commanded the blessing, even life forevermore [upon the high and the lowly].

PSALM 134

A Song of Ascents.

¹BEHOLD, BLESS (affectionately and gratefully praise) the Lord, all you servants of the Lord, [singers] who by night stand in the house of the Lord.

²Lift up your hands in holiness and to the sanctuary and bless the Lord [affectionately and gratefully praise Him]!

³The Lord bless you out of Zion, even He Who made heaven and earth.

PSALM 135

¹PRAISE THE Lord! (Hallelujah!) Praise the name of the Lord; praise Him, O you servants of the Lord!

²You who stand in the house of the Lord, in the courts of the house of our God,

³Praise the Lord! For the Lord is good; sing praises to His name, for He is gracious and lovely!

⁴For the Lord has chosen [the descendants of] Jacob for Himself, Israel for His peculiar possession and treasure.

⁵For I know that the Lord is great and that our Lord is above all gods.

⁶Whatever the Lord pleases, that has He done in the heavens and on earth, in the seas and all deeps--

⁷Who causes the vapors to arise from the ends of the earth, Who makes lightnings for the rain, Who brings the wind out of His storehouses;

⁸Who smote the firstborn of Egypt, both of man and beast;

⁹Who sent signs and wonders into the midst of you, O Egypt, upon Pharaoh and all his servants;

¹⁰Who smote nations many and great and slew mighty kings--

¹¹Sihon king of the Amorites, Og king of Bashan, and all the kingdoms of Canaan.

¹²[The Lord] gave their land as a heritage, a heritage to Israel His people.

¹³Your name, O Lord, endures forever, Your fame, O Lord, throughout all ages.

¹⁴For the Lord will judge and vindicate His people, and He will delay His judgments [manifesting His righteousness and mercy] and take into favor His servants [those who meet His terms of separation unto Him].

¹⁵The idols of the nations are silver and gold, the work of men's hands.

¹⁶[Idols] have mouths, but they speak not; eyes have they, but they see not;

¹⁷They have ears, but they hear not, nor is there any breath in their mouths.

¹⁸Those who make [idols] are like them; so is everyone who trusts in and relies on them.

¹⁹Bless (affectionately and gratefully praise) the Lord, O house of Israel; bless the Lord, O house of Aaron [God's ministers].

²⁰Bless the Lord, O house of Levi [the dedicated tribe]; you who reverently and worshipfully fear the Lord, bless the Lord [affectionately and gratefully praise Him]!

²¹Blessed out of Zion be the Lord, Who dwells [with us] at Jerusalem! Praise the Lord! (Hallelujah!)

PSALM 136

¹O GIVE thanks to the Lord, for He is good; for His mercy and loving-kindness endure forever.

²O give thanks to the God of gods, for His mercy and loving-kindness endure forever.

[3]O give thanks to the Lord of lords, for His mercy and loving-kindness endure forever--

[4]To Him Who alone does great wonders, for His mercy and loving-kindness endure forever;

[5]To Him Who by wisdom and understanding made the heavens, for His mercy and loving-kindness endure forever;

[6]To Him Who stretched out the earth upon the waters, for His mercy and loving-kindness endure forever;

[7]To Him Who made the great lights, for His mercy and loving-kindness endure forever--

[8]The sun to rule over the day, for His mercy and loving-kindness endure forever;

[9]The moon and stars to rule by night, for His mercy and loving-kindness endure forever;

[10]To Him Who smote Egypt in their firstborn, for His mercy and loving-kindness endure forever;

[11]And brought out Israel from among them, for His mercy and loving-kindness endure forever;

[12]With a strong hand and with an outstretched arm, for His mercy and loving-kindness endure forever;

[13]To Him Who divided the Red Sea into parts, for His mercy and loving-kindness endure forever;

[14]And made Israel to pass through the midst of it, for His mercy and loving-kindness endure forever;

[15]But shook off and overthrew Pharaoh and his host into the Red Sea, for His mercy and loving-kindness endure forever;

[16]To Him Who led His people through the wilderness, for His mercy and loving-kindness endure forever;

[17]To Him Who smote great kings, for His mercy and loving-kindness endure forever;

[18]And slew famous kings, for His mercy and loving-kindness endure forever--

[19]Sihon king of the Amorites, for His mercy and loving-kindness endure forever;

[20]And Og king of Bashan, for His mercy and loving-kindness endure forever;

[21]And gave their land as a heritage, for His mercy and loving-kindness endure forever;

²²Even a heritage to Israel His servant, for His mercy and loving-kindness endure forever;

²³To Him Who [earnestly] remembered us in our low estate and imprinted us [on His heart], for His mercy and loving-kindness endure forever;

²⁴And rescued us from our enemies, for His mercy and loving-kindness endure forever;

²⁵To Him Who gives food to all flesh, for His mercy and loving-kindness endure forever;

²⁶O give thanks to the God of heaven, for His mercy and loving-kindness endure forever!

PSALM 137

¹BY THE rivers of Babylon, there we [captives] sat down, yes, we wept when we [earnestly] remembered Zion [the city of our God imprinted on our hearts].

²On the willow trees in the midst of [Babylon] we hung our harps.

³For there they who led us captive required of us a song with words, and our tormentors and they who wasted us required of us mirth, saying, Sing us one of the songs of Zion.

⁴How shall we sing the Lord's song in a strange land?

⁵If I forget you, O Jerusalem, let my right hand forget its skill [with the harp].

⁶Let my tongue cleave to the roof of my mouth if I remember you not, if I prefer not Jerusalem above my chief joy!

⁷Remember, O Lord, against the Edomites, that they said in the day of Jerusalem's fall, Down, down to the ground with her!

⁸O Daughter of Babylon [you devastator, you!], who [ought to be and] shall be destroyed, happy and blessed shall he be who requites you as you have served us.

⁹Happy and blessed shall he be who takes and dashes your little ones against the rock!

PSALM 138

¹I WILL confess and praise You [O God] with my whole heart; before the gods will I sing praises to You.

²I will worship toward Your holy temple and praise Your name for Your loving-kindness and for Your truth and faithfulness; for You have exalted above all else Your name and Your word and You have magnified Your word above all Your name!

³In the day when I called, You answered me; and You strengthened me with strength (might and inflexibility to temptation) in my inner self.

⁴All the kings of the land shall give You credit and praise You, O Lord, for they have heard of the promises of Your mouth [which were fulfilled].

⁵Yes, they shall sing of the ways of the Lord and joyfully celebrate His mighty acts, for great is the glory of the Lord.

⁶For though the Lord is high, yet has He respect to the lowly [bringing them into fellowship with Him]; but the proud and haughty He knows and recognizes [only] at a distance.

⁷Though I walk in the midst of trouble, You will revive me; You will stretch forth Your hand against the wrath of my enemies, and Your right hand will save me.

⁸The Lord will perfect that which concerns me; Your mercy and loving-kindness, O Lord, endure forever--forsake not the works of Your own hands.

PSALM 139

To the Chief Musician. A Psalm of David.

¹O LORD, you have searched me [thoroughly] and have known me.

²You know my downsitting and my uprising; You understand my thought afar off.

³You sift and search out my path and my lying down, and You are acquainted with all my ways.

⁴For there is not a word in my tongue [still unuttered], but, behold, O Lord, You know it altogether.

⁵You have beset me and shut me in--behind and before, and You have laid Your hand upon me.

⁶Your [infinite] knowledge is too wonderful for me; it is high above me, I cannot reach it.

⁷Where could I go from Your Spirit? Or where could I flee from Your presence?

⁸If I ascend up into heaven, You are there; if I make my bed in Sheol (the grave), behold, You are there.

⁹If I take the wings of the morning or dwell in the uttermost parts of the sea,

¹⁰Even there shall Your hand lead me, and Your right hand shall hold me.

¹¹If I say, Surely the darkness shall cover me and the night shall be [the only] light about me,

¹²Even the darkness hides nothing from You, but the night shines as the day; the darkness and the light are both alike to You.

¹³For You did form my inward parts; You did knit me together in my mother's womb.

¹⁴I will confess and praise You for You are fearful and wonderful and for the awful wonder of my birth! Wonderful are Your works, and that my inner self knows right well.

¹⁵My frame was not hidden from You when I was being formed in secret [and] intricately and curiously wrought [as if embroidered with various colors] in the depths of the earth [a region of darkness and mystery].

¹⁶Your eyes saw my unformed substance, and in Your book all the days [of my life] were written before ever they took shape, when as yet there was none of them.

¹⁷How precious and weighty also are Your thoughts to me, O God! How vast is the sum of them!

¹⁸If I could count them, they would be more in number than the sand. When I awoke, [could I count to the end] I would still be with You.

¹⁹If You would [only] slay the wicked, O God, and the men of blood depart from me--

²⁰Who speak against You wickedly, Your enemies who take Your name in vain!

²¹Do I not hate them, O Lord, who hate You? And am I not grieved and do I not loathe those who rise up against You?

²²I hate them with perfect hatred; they have become my enemies.

²³Search me [thoroughly], O God, and know my heart! Try me and know my thoughts!

²⁴And see if there is any wicked or hurtful way in me, and lead me in the way everlasting.

PSALM 140

To the Chief Musician. A Psalm of David.

¹DELIVER ME, O Lord, from evil men; preserve me from violent men;

²They devise mischiefs in their heart; continually they gather together and stir up wars.

³They sharpen their tongues like a serpent's; adders' poison is under their lips. Selah [pause, and calmly think of that]!

⁴Keep me, O Lord, from the hands of the wicked; preserve me from the violent men who have purposed to thrust aside my steps.

⁵The proud have hidden a snare for me; they have spread cords as a net by the wayside, they have set traps for me. Selah [pause, and calmly think of that]!

⁶I said to the Lord, You are my God; give ear to the voice of my supplications, O Lord.

⁷O God the Lord, the Strength of my salvation, You have covered my head in the day of battle.

⁸Grant not, O Lord, the desires of the wicked; further not their wicked plot and device, lest they exalt themselves. Selah [pause, and calmly think of that]!

⁹Those who are fencing me in raise their heads; may the mischief of their own lips and the very things they desire for me come upon them.

¹⁰Let burning coals fall upon them; let them be cast into the fire, into floods of water or deep water pits, from which they shall not rise.

¹¹Let not a man of slanderous tongue be established in the earth; let evil hunt the violent man to overthrow him [let calamity follow his evildoings].

¹²I know and rest in confidence upon it that the Lord will maintain the cause of the afflicted, and will secure justice for the poor and needy [of His believing children].

¹³Surely the [uncompromisingly] righteous shall give thanks to Your name; the upright shall dwell in Your presence (before Your very face).

PSALM 141

A Psalm of David.

¹LORD, I call upon You; hasten to me. Give ear to my voice when I cry to You.

²Let my prayer be set forth as incense before You, the lifting up of my hands as the evening sacrifice.

³Set a guard, O Lord, before my mouth; keep watch at the door of my lips.

⁴Incline my heart not to submit or consent to any evil thing or to be occupied in deeds of wickedness with men who work iniquity; and let me not eat of their dainties.

⁵Let the righteous man smite and correct me--it is a kindness. Oil so choice let not my head refuse or discourage; for even in their evils or calamities shall my prayer continue.

⁶When their rulers are overthrown in stony places, [their followers] shall hear my words, that they are sweet (pleasant, mild, and just).

⁷The unburied bones [of slaughtered rulers] shall lie scattered at the mouth of Sheol, [as unregarded] as the lumps of soil behind the plowman when he breaks open the ground.

⁸But my eyes are toward You, O God the Lord; in You do I trust and take refuge; pour not out my life nor leave it destitute and bare.

⁹Keep me from the trap which they have laid for me, and the snares of evildoers.

¹⁰Let the wicked fall together into their own nets, while I pass over them and escape.

PSALM 142

A skillful song, or a didactic or reflective poem, of David; when he was in the cave. A Prayer.

¹I CRY to the Lord with my voice; with my voice to the Lord do I make supplication.

²I pour out my complaint before Him; I tell before Him my trouble.

³When my spirit was overwhelmed and fainted [throwing all its weight] upon me, then You knew my path. In the way where I walk they have hidden a snare for me.

⁴Look on the right hand [the point of attack] and see; for there is no man who knows me [to appear for me]. Refuge has failed me and I have no way to flee; no man cares for my life or my welfare.

⁵I cried to You, O Lord; I said, You are my refuge, my portion in the land of the living.

⁶Attend to my loud cry, for I am brought very low; deliver me from my persecutors, for they are stronger than I.

⁷Bring my life out of prison, that I may confess, praise, and give thanks to Your name; the righteous will surround me and crown themselves because of me, for You will deal bountifully with me.

PSALM 143
A Psalm of David.

¹HEAR MY prayer, O Lord, give ear to my supplications! In Your faithfulness answer me, and in Your righteousness.

²And enter not into judgment with Your servant, for in Your sight no man living is [in himself] righteous or justified.

³For the enemy has pursued and persecuted my soul, he has crushed my life down to the ground; he has made me to dwell in dark places as those who have been long dead.

⁴Therefore is my spirit overwhelmed and faints within me [wrapped in gloom]; my heart within my bosom grows numb.

⁵I remember the days of old; I meditate on all Your doings; I ponder the work of Your hands.

⁶I spread forth my hands to You; my soul thirsts after You like a thirsty land [for water]. Selah [pause, and calmly think of that]!

⁷Answer me speedily, O Lord, for my spirit fails; hide not Your face from me, lest I become like those who go down into the pit (the grave).

⁸Cause me to hear Your loving-kindness in the morning, for on You do I lean and in You do I trust. Cause me to know the way wherein I should walk, for I lift up my inner self to You.

⁹Deliver me, O Lord, from my enemies; I flee to You to hide me.

¹⁰Teach me to do Your will, for You are my God; let Your good Spirit lead me into a level country and into the land of uprightness.

¹¹Save my life, O Lord, for Your name's sake; in Your righteousness, bring my life out of trouble and free me from distress.

¹²And in your mercy and loving-kindness, cut off my enemies and destroy all those who afflict my inner self, for I am Your servant.

PSALM 144

[A Psalm] of David.

¹BLESSED BE the Lord, my Rock and my keen and firm Strength, Who teaches my hands to war and my fingers to fight--

²My Steadfast Love and my Fortress, my High Tower and my Deliverer, my Shield and He in Whom I trust and take refuge, Who subdues my people under me.

³Lord, what is man that You take notice of him? Or [the] son of man that You take account of him?

⁴Man is like vanity and a breath; his days are as a shadow that passes away.

⁵Bow Your heavens, O Lord, and come down; touch the mountains, and they shall smoke.

⁶Cast forth lightning and scatter [my enemies]; send out Your arrows and embarrass and frustrate them.

⁷Stretch forth Your hand from above; rescue me and deliver me out of great waters, from the hands of hostile aliens (tribes around us)

⁸Whose mouths speak deceit and whose right hands are right hands [raised in taking] fraudulent oaths.

⁹I will sing a new song to You, O God; upon a harp, an instrument of ten strings, will I offer praises to You.

¹⁰You are He Who gives salvation to kings, Who rescues David His servant from the hurtful sword [of evil].

¹¹Rescue me and deliver me out of the power of [hostile] alien [tribes] whose mouths speak deceit and whose right hands are right hands [raised in taking] fraudulent oaths.

¹²When our sons shall be as plants grown large in their youth and our daughters as sculptured corner pillars hewn like those of a palace;

¹³When our garners are full, affording all manner of store, and our sheep bring forth thousands and ten thousands in our pastures;

¹⁴When our oxen are well loaded; when there is no invasion [of hostile armies] and no going forth [against besiegers--when there is no murder or manslaughter] and no outcry in our streets;

¹⁵Happy and blessed are the people who are in such a case; yes, happy (blessed, fortunate, prosperous, to be envied) are the people whose God is the Lord!

PSALM 145

[A Psalm] of praise. Of David.

¹I WILL extol You, my God, O King; and I will bless Your name forever and ever [with grateful, affectionate praise].

²Every day [with its new reasons] will I bless You [affectionately and gratefully praise You]; yes, I will praise Your name forever and ever.

³Great is the Lord and highly to be praised; and His greatness is [so vast and deep as to be] unsearchable.

⁴One generation shall laud Your works to another and shall declare Your mighty acts.

⁵On the glorious splendor of Your majesty and on Your wondrous works I will meditate.

⁶Men shall speak of the might of Your tremendous and terrible acts, and I will declare Your greatness.

⁷They shall pour forth [like a fountain] the fame of Your great and abundant goodness and shall sing aloud of Your rightness and justice.

⁸The Lord is gracious and full of compassion, slow to anger and abounding in mercy and loving-kindness.

⁹The Lord is good to all, and His tender mercies are over all His works [the entirety of things created].

¹⁰All Your works shall praise You, O Lord, and Your loving ones shall bless You [affectionately and gratefully shall Your saints confess and praise You]!

¹¹They shall speak of the glory of Your kingdom and talk of Your power,

¹²To make known to the sons of men God's mighty deeds and the glorious majesty of His kingdom.

¹³Your kingdom is an everlasting kingdom, and Your dominion endures throughout all generations.

¹⁴The Lord upholds all those [of His own] who are falling and raises up all those who are bowed down.

¹⁵The eyes of all wait for You [looking, watching, and expecting] and You give them their food in due season.

¹⁶You open Your hand and satisfy every living thing with favor.

¹⁷The Lord is [rigidly] righteous in all His ways and gracious and merciful in all His works.

¹⁸The Lord is near to all who call upon Him, to all who call upon Him sincerely and in truth.

¹⁹He will fulfill the desires of those who reverently and worshipfully fear Him; He also will hear their cry and will save them.

²⁰The Lord preserves all those who love Him, but all the wicked will He destroy.

²¹My mouth shall speak the praise of the Lord; and let all flesh bless (affectionately and gratefully praise) His holy name forever and ever.

PSALM 146

¹PRAISE THE Lord! (Hallelujah!) Praise the Lord, O my soul!

²While I live will I praise the Lord; I will sing praises to my God while I have any being.

³Put not your trust in princes, in a son of man, in whom there is no help.

⁴When his breath leaves him, he returns to his earth; in that very day his [previous] thoughts, plans, and purposes perish.

⁵Happy (blessed, fortunate, enviable) is he who has the God of [special revelation to] Jacob for his help, whose hope is in the Lord his God,

⁶Who made heaven and earth, the sea, and all that is in them, Who keeps truth and is faithful forever,

⁷Who executes justice for the oppressed, Who gives food to the hungry. The Lord sets free the prisoners,

⁸The Lord opens the eyes of the blind, the Lord lifts up those who are bowed down, the Lord loves the [uncompromisingly] righteous (those upright in heart and in right standing with Him).

⁹The Lord protects and preserves the strangers and temporary residents, He upholds the fatherless and the widow and sets them upright, but the way of the wicked He makes crooked (turns upside down and brings to ruin).

¹⁰The Lord shall reign forever, even Your God, O Zion, from generation to generation. Praise the Lord! (Hallelujah!)

PSALM 147

¹PRAISE THE Lord! For it is good to sing praises to our God, for He is gracious and lovely; praise is becoming and appropriate.

²The Lord is building up Jerusalem; He is gathering together the exiles of Israel.

³He heals the brokenhearted and binds up their wounds [curing their pains and their sorrows].

⁴He determines and counts the number of the stars; He calls them all by their names.

⁵Great is our Lord and of great power; His understanding is inexhaustible and boundless.

⁶The Lord lifts up the humble and downtrodden; He casts the wicked down to the ground.

⁷Sing to the Lord with thanksgiving; sing praises with the harp or the lyre to our God!--

⁸Who covers the heavens with clouds, Who prepares rain for the earth, Who makes grass to grow on the mountains.

⁹He gives to the beast his food, and to the young ravens that for which they cry.

¹⁰He delights not in the strength of the horse, nor does He take pleasure in the legs of a man.

¹¹The Lord takes pleasure in those who reverently and worshipfully fear Him, in those who hope in His mercy and loving-kindness.

¹²Praise the Lord, O Jerusalem! Praise your God, O Zion!

¹³For He has strengthened and made hard the bars of your gates, and He has blessed your children within you.

¹⁴He makes peace in your borders; He fills you with the finest of the wheat.

¹⁵He sends forth His commandment to the earth; His word runs very swiftly.

¹⁶He gives [to the earth] snow like [a blanket of] wool; He scatters the hoarfrost like ashes.

¹⁷He casts forth His ice like crumbs; who can stand before His cold?

¹⁸He sends out His word, and melts [ice and snow]; He causes His wind to blow, and the waters flow.

¹⁹He declares His word to Jacob, His statutes and His ordinances to Israel.

²⁰He has not dealt so with any [other] nation; they have not known (understood, appreciated, given heed to, and cherished) His ordinances. Praise the Lord! (Hallelujah!)

PSALM 148

¹PRAISE THE Lord! Praise the Lord from the heavens, praise Him in the heights!

²Praise Him, all His angels, praise Him, all His hosts!

³Praise Him, sun and moon, praise Him, all you stars of light!

⁴Praise Him, you highest heavens and you waters above the heavens!

⁵Let them praise the name of the Lord, for He commanded and they were created.

⁶He also established them forever and ever; He made a decree which shall not pass away [He fixed their bounds which cannot be passed over].

⁷Praise the Lord from the earth, you sea monsters and all deeps!

⁸You lightning, hail, fog, and frost, you stormy wind fulfilling His orders!

⁹Mountains and all hills, fruitful trees and all cedars!

¹⁰Beasts and all cattle, creeping things and flying birds!

¹¹Kings of the earth and all peoples, princes and all rulers and judges of the earth!

¹²Both young men and maidens, old men and children!

¹³Let them praise and exalt the name of the Lord, for His name alone is exalted and supreme! His glory and majesty are above earth and heaven!

¹⁴He has lifted up a horn for His people [giving them power, prosperity, dignity, and preeminence], a song of praise for all His godly ones, for the people of Israel, who are near to Him. Praise the Lord! (Hallelujah!)

PSALM 149

¹PRAISE THE Lord! Sing to the Lord a new song, praise Him in the assembly of His saints!

²Let Israel rejoice in Him, their Maker; let Zion's children triumph and be joyful in their King!

³Let them praise His name in chorus and choir and with the [single or group] dance; let them sing praises to Him with the tambourine and lyre!

[4]For the Lord takes pleasure in His people; He will beautify the humble with salvation and adorn the wretched with victory.

[5]Let the saints be joyful in the glory and beauty [which God confers upon them]; let them sing for joy upon their beds.

[6]Let the high praises of God be in their throats and a two-edged sword in their hands,

[7]To wreak vengeance upon the nations and chastisement upon the peoples,

[8]To bind their kings with chains, and their nobles with fetters of iron,

[9]To execute upon them the judgment written. He [the Lord] is the honor of all His saints. Praise the Lord! (Hallelujah!)

PSALM 150

[1]PRAISE THE Lord! Praise God in His sanctuary; praise Him in the heavens of His power!

[2]Praise Him for His mighty acts; praise Him according to the abundance of His greatness!

[3]Praise Him with trumpet sound; praise Him with lute and harp!

[4]Praise Him with tambourine and [single or group] dance; praise Him with stringed and wind instruments or flutes!

[5]Praise Him with resounding cymbals; praise Him with loud clashing cymbals!

[6]Let everything that has breath and every breath of life praise the Lord! Praise the Lord! (Hallelujah!)

Proverbs

PROVERBS 1

¹THE PROVERBS (truths obscurely expressed, maxims, and parables) of Solomon son of David, king of Israel:

²That people may know skillful and godly Wisdom and instruction, discern and comprehend the words of understanding and insight,

³Receive instruction in wise dealing and the discipline of wise thoughtfulness, righteousness, justice, and integrity,

⁴That prudence may be given to the simple, and knowledge, discretion, and discernment to the youth--

⁵The wise also will hear and increase in learning, and the person of understanding will acquire skill and attain to sound counsel--

⁶That people may understand a proverb and a figure of speech or an enigma with its interpretation, and the words of the wise and their dark sayings or riddles.

⁷The reverent and worshipful fear of the Lord is the beginning and the principal and choice part of knowledge [its starting point and its essence]; but fools despise skillful and godly Wisdom, instruction, and discipline.

⁸My son, hear the instruction of your father; reject not nor forsake the teaching of your mother.

⁹For they are a [victor's] chaplet (garland) of grace upon your head and chains and pendants [of gold worn by kings] for your neck.

¹⁰My son, if sinners entice you, do not consent.

¹¹If they say, Come with us; let us lie in wait [to shed] blood, let us ambush the innocent without cause [and show that his piety is in vain];

¹²Let us swallow them up alive as does Sheol (grave), and whole, as those who go down into the pit [grave];

¹³We shall find and take all kinds of precious goods [when our victims are put out of the way], we shall fill our houses with plunder;

¹⁴Throw in your lot with us [they insist] and be a sworn brother and comrade; let us all have one purse in common--

¹⁵My son, do not walk in the way with them; restrain your foot from their path;

¹⁶For their feet run to evil, and they make haste to shed blood.

¹⁷For in vain is the net spread in the sight of any bird!

¹⁸But [when these men set a trap for others] they are lying in wait for their own blood; they set an ambush for their own lives.

¹⁹So are the ways of everyone who is greedy of gain; such [greed] takes away the lives of its possessors.

²⁰Wisdom cries aloud in the street, she raises her voice in the markets;

²¹She cries at the head of the noisy intersections [in the chief gathering places]; at the entrance of the city gates she speaks:

²²How long, O simple ones [open to evil], will you love being simple? And the scoffers delight in scoffing and [self-confident] fools hate knowledge?

²³If you will turn (repent) and give heed to my reproof, behold, I [Wisdom] will pour out my spirit upon you, I will make my words known to you.

²⁴Because I have called and you have refused [to answer], have stretched out my hand and no man has heeded it,

²⁵And you treated as nothing all my counsel and would accept none of my reproof,

²⁶I also will laugh at your calamity; I will mock when the thing comes that shall cause you terror and panic--

²⁷When your panic comes as a storm and desolation and your calamity comes on as a whirlwind, when distress and anguish come upon you.

²⁸Then will they call upon me [Wisdom] but I will not answer; they will seek me early and diligently but they will not find me.

²⁹Because they hated knowledge and did not choose the reverent and worshipful fear of the Lord,

³⁰Would accept none of my counsel, and despised all my reproof,

³¹Therefore shall they eat of the fruit of their own way and be satiated with their own devices.

³²For the backsliding of the simple shall slay them, and the careless ease of [self-confident] fools shall destroy them.

³³But whoso hearkens to me [Wisdom] shall dwell securely and in confident trust and shall be quiet, without fear or dread of evil.

PROVERBS 2

¹MY SON, if you will receive my words and treasure up my commandments within you,

²Making your ear attentive to skillful and godly Wisdom and inclining and directing your heart and mind to understanding [applying all your powers to the quest for it];

³Yes, if you cry out for insight and raise your voice for understanding,

⁴If you seek [Wisdom] as for silver and search for skillful and godly Wisdom as for hidden treasures,

⁵Then you will understand the reverent and worshipful fear of the Lord and find the knowledge of [our omniscient] God.

⁶For the Lord gives skillful and godly Wisdom; from His mouth come knowledge and understanding.

⁷He hides away sound and godly Wisdom and stores it for the righteous (those who are upright and in right standing with Him); He is a shield to those who walk uprightly and in integrity,

⁸That He may guard the paths of justice; yes, He preserves the way of His saints.

⁹Then you will understand righteousness, justice, and fair dealing [in every area and relation]; yes, you will understand every good path.

¹⁰For skillful and godly Wisdom shall enter into your heart, and knowledge shall be pleasant to you.

¹¹Discretion shall watch over you, understanding shall keep you,

¹²To deliver you from the way of evil and the evil men, from men who speak perverse things and are liars,

¹³Men who forsake the paths of uprightness to walk in the ways of darkness,

¹⁴Who rejoice to do evil and delight in the perverseness of evil,

¹⁵Who are crooked in their ways, wayward and devious in their paths.

¹⁶[Discretion shall watch over you, understanding shall keep you] to deliver you from the alien woman, from the outsider with her flattering words,

¹⁷Who forsakes the husband and guide of her youth and forgets the covenant of her God.

¹⁸For her house sinks down to death and her paths to the spirits [of the dead].

¹⁹None who go to her return again, neither do they attain or regain the paths of life.

²⁰So may you walk in the way of good men, and keep to the paths of the [consistently] righteous (the upright, in right standing with God).

²¹For the upright shall dwell in the land, and the men of integrity, blameless and complete [in God's sight], shall remain in it;

²²But the wicked shall be cut off from the earth, and the treacherous shall be rooted out of it.

PROVERBS 3

¹MY SON, forget not my law or teaching, but let your heart keep my commandments;

²For length of days and years of a life [worth living] and tranquility [inward and outward and continuing through old age till death], these shall they add to you.

³Let not mercy and kindness [shutting out all hatred and selfishness] and truth [shutting out all deliberate hypocrisy or falsehood] forsake you; bind them about your neck, write them upon the tablet of your heart.

⁴So shall you find favor, good understanding, and high esteem in the sight [or judgment] of God and man.

⁵Lean on, trust in, and be confident in the Lord with all your heart and mind and do not rely on your own insight or understanding.

⁶In all your ways know, recognize, and acknowledge Him, and He will direct and make straight and plain your paths.

⁷Be not wise in your own eyes; reverently fear and worship the Lord and turn [entirely] away from evil.

⁸It shall be health to your nerves and sinews, and marrow and moistening to your bones.

⁹Honor the Lord with your capital and sufficiency [from righteous labors] and with the firstfruits of all your income;

¹⁰So shall your storage places be filled with plenty, and your vats shall be overflowing with new wine.

¹¹My son, do not despise or shrink from the chastening of the Lord [His correction by punishment or by subjection to suffering or trial]; neither be weary of or impatient about or loathe or abhor His reproof,

¹²For whom the Lord loves He corrects, even as a father corrects the son in whom he delights.

¹³Happy (blessed, fortunate, enviable) is the man who finds skillful and godly Wisdom, and the man who gets understanding [drawing it forth from God's Word and life's experiences],

¹⁴For the gaining of it is better than the gaining of silver, and the profit of it better than fine gold.

¹⁵Skillful and godly Wisdom is more precious than rubies; and nothing you can wish for is to be compared to her.

¹⁶Length of days is in her right hand, and in her left hand are riches and honor.

¹⁷Her ways are highways of pleasantness, and all her paths are peace.

¹⁸She is a tree of life to those who lay hold on her; and happy (blessed, fortunate, to be envied) is everyone who holds her fast.

¹⁹The Lord by skillful and godly Wisdom has founded the earth; by understanding He has established the heavens.

²⁰By His knowledge the deeps were broken up, and the skies distill the dew.

²¹My son, let them not escape from your sight, but keep sound and godly Wisdom and discretion,

²²And they will be life to your inner self, and a gracious ornament to your neck (your outer self).

²³Then you will walk in your way securely and in confident trust, and you shall not dash your foot or stumble.

²⁴When you lie down, you shall not be afraid; yes, you shall lie down, and your sleep shall be sweet.

²⁵Be not afraid of sudden terror and panic, nor of the stormy blast or the storm and ruin of the wicked when it comes [for you will be guiltless],

²⁶For the Lord shall be your confidence, firm and strong, and shall keep your foot from being caught [in a trap or some hidden danger].

²⁷Withhold not good from those to whom it is due [its rightful owners], when it is in the power of your hand to do it.

²⁸Do not say to your neighbor, Go, and come again; and tomorrow I will give it--when you have it with you.

²⁹Do not contrive or dig up or cultivate evil against your neighbor, who dwells trustingly and confidently beside you.

³⁰Contend not with a man for no reason--when he has done you no wrong.

³¹Do not resentfully envy and be jealous of an unscrupulous, grasping man, and choose none of his ways.

³²For the perverse are an abomination [extremely disgusting and detestable] to the Lord; but His confidential communion and secret counsel are with the [uncompromisingly] righteous (those who are upright and in right standing with Him).

³³The curse of the Lord is in and on the house of the wicked, but He declares blessed (joyful and favored with blessings) the home of the just and consistently righteous.

³⁴Though He scoffs at the scoffers and scorns the scorners, yet He gives His undeserved favor to the low [in rank], the humble, and the afflicted.

³⁵The wise shall inherit glory (all honor and good) but shame is the highest rank conferred on [self-confident] fools.

PROVERBS 4

¹HEAR, MY sons, the instruction of a father, and pay attention in order to gain and to know intelligent discernment, comprehension, and interpretation [of spiritual matters].

²For I give you good doctrine [what is to be received]; do not forsake my teaching.

³When I [Solomon] was a son with my father [David], tender and the only son in the sight of my mother [Bathsheba],

⁴He taught me and said to me, Let your heart hold fast my words; keep my commandments and live.

⁵Get skillful and godly Wisdom, get understanding (discernment, comprehension, and interpretation); do not forget and do not turn back from the words of my mouth.

⁶Forsake not [Wisdom], and she will keep, defend, and protect you; love her, and she will guard you.

⁷The beginning of Wisdom is: get Wisdom (skillful and godly Wisdom)! [For skillful and godly Wisdom is the principal thing.] And with all you have gotten, get understanding (discernment, comprehension, and interpretation).

⁸Prize Wisdom highly and exalt her, and she will exalt and promote you; she will bring you to honor when you embrace her.

⁹She shall give to your head a wreath of gracefulness; a crown of beauty and glory will she deliver to you.

¹⁰Hear, O my son, and receive my sayings, and the years of your life shall be many.

¹¹I have taught you in the way of skillful and godly Wisdom [comprehensive insight into the ways of God]; I have led you in paths of uprightness.

¹²When you walk, your steps shall not be hampered [your path will be clear]; and when you run, you shall not stumble.

¹³Take firm hold of instruction, do not let go; guard her, for she is your life.

¹⁴Enter not into the path of the wicked, and go not in the way of evil men.

¹⁵Avoid it, do not go on it; turn from it and pass on.

¹⁶For they cannot sleep unless they have caused trouble or vexation; their sleep is taken away unless they have caused someone to fall.

¹⁷For they eat the bread of wickedness and drink the wine of violence.

¹⁸But the path of the [uncompromisingly] just and righteous is like the light of dawn, that shines more and more (brighter and clearer) until [it reaches its full strength and glory in] the perfect day [to be prepared].

¹⁹The way of the wicked is like deep darkness; they do not know over what they stumble.

²⁰My son, attend to my words; consent and submit to my sayings.

²¹Let them not depart from your sight; keep them in the center of your heart.

²²For they are life to those who find them, healing and health to all their flesh.

²³Keep and guard your heart with all vigilance and above all that you guard, for out of it flow the springs of life.

²⁴Put away from you false and dishonest speech, and willful and contrary talk put far from you.

²⁵Let your eyes look right on [with fixed purpose], and let your gaze be straight before you.

²⁶Consider well the path of your feet, and let all your ways be established and ordered aright.

²⁷Turn not aside to the right hand or to the left; remove your foot from evil.

PROVERBS 5

¹MY SON, be attentive to my Wisdom [godly Wisdom learned by actual and costly experience], and incline your ear to my understanding [of what is becoming and prudent for you],

²That you may exercise proper discrimination and discretion and your lips may guard and keep knowledge and the wise answer [to temptation].

³For the lips of a loose woman drip honey as a honeycomb, and her mouth is smoother than oil;

⁴But in the end she is bitter as wormwood, sharp as a two-edged and devouring sword.

⁵Her feet go down to death; her steps take hold of Sheol (Hades, the place of the dead).

⁶She loses sight of and walks not in the path of life; her ways wind about aimlessly, and you cannot know them.

⁷Now therefore, my sons, listen to me, and depart not from the words of my mouth.

⁸Let your way in life be far from her, and come not near the door of her house [avoid the very scenes of temptation],

⁹Lest you give your honor to others and your years to those without mercy,

¹⁰Lest strangers [and false teachings] take their fill of your strength and wealth and your labors go to the house of an alien [from God]--

¹¹And you groan and mourn when your end comes, when your flesh and body are consumed,

¹²And you say, How I hated instruction and discipline, and my heart despised reproof!

¹³I have not obeyed the voice of my teachers nor submitted and consented to those who instructed me.

¹⁴[The extent and boldness of] my sin involved almost all evil [in the estimation] of the congregation and the community.

¹⁵Drink waters out of your own cistern [of a pure marriage relationship], and fresh running waters out of your own well.

¹⁶Should your offspring be dispersed abroad as water brooks in the streets?

¹⁷[Confine yourself to your own wife] let your children be for you alone, and not the children of strangers with you.

¹⁸Let your fountain [of human life] be blessed [with the rewards of fidelity], and rejoice in the wife of your youth.

[19]Let her be as the loving hind and pleasant doe [tender, gentle, attractive]--let her bosom satisfy you at all times, and always be transported with delight in her love.

[20]Why should you, my son, be infatuated with a loose woman, embrace the bosom of an outsider, and go astray?

[21]For the ways of man are directly before the eyes of the Lord, and He [Who would have us live soberly, chastely, and godly] carefully weighs all man's goings.

[22]His own iniquities shall ensnare the wicked man, and he shall be held with the cords of his sin.

[23]He will die for lack of discipline and instruction, and in the greatness of his folly he will go astray and be lost.

PROVERBS 6

[1]MY SON, if you have become security for your neighbor, if you have given your pledge for a stranger or another,

[2]You are snared with the words of your lips, you are caught by the speech of your mouth.

[3]Do this now [at once and earnestly], my son, and deliver yourself when you have put yourself into the power of your neighbor; go, bestir and humble yourself, and beg your neighbor [to pay his debt and thereby release you].

[4]Give not [unnecessary] sleep to your eyes, nor slumber to your eyelids;

[5]Deliver yourself, as a roe or gazelle from the hand of the hunter, and as a bird from the hand of the fowler.

[6]Go to the ant, you sluggard; consider her ways and be wise!--

[7]Which, having no chief, overseer, or ruler,

[8]Provides her food in the summer and gathers her supplies in the harvest.

[9]How long will you sleep, O sluggard? When will you arise out of your sleep?

[10]Yet a little sleep, a little slumber, a little folding of the hands to lie down and sleep--

[11]So will your poverty come like a robber or one who travels [with slowly but surely approaching steps] and your want like an armed man [making you helpless].

¹²A worthless person, a wicked man, is he who goes about with a perverse (contrary, wayward) mouth.

¹³He winks with his eyes, he speaks by shuffling or tapping with his feet, he makes signs [to mislead and deceive] and teaches with his fingers.

¹⁴Willful and contrary in his heart, he devises trouble, vexation, and evil continually; he lets loose discord and sows it.

¹⁵Therefore upon him shall the crushing weight of calamity come suddenly; suddenly shall he be broken, and that without remedy.

¹⁶These six things the Lord hates, indeed, seven are an abomination to Him:

¹⁷A proud look, a lying tongue, and hands that shed innocent blood,

¹⁸A heart that manufactures wicked thoughts and plans, feet that are swift in running to evil,

¹⁹A false witness who breathes out lies [even under oath], and he who sows discord among his brethren.

²⁰My son, keep your father's [God-given] commandment and forsake not the law of [God] your mother [taught you].

²¹Bind them continually upon your heart and tie them about your neck.

²²When you go, they [the words of your parents' God] shall lead you; when you sleep, they shall keep you; and when you waken, they shall talk with you.

²³For the commandment is a lamp, and the whole teaching [of the law] is light, and reproofs of discipline are the way of life,

²⁴To keep you from the evil woman, from the flattery of the tongue of a loose woman.

²⁵Lust not after her beauty in your heart, neither let her capture you with her eyelids.

²⁶For on account of a harlot a man is brought to a piece of bread, and the adulteress stalks and snares [as with a hook] the precious life [of a man].

²⁷Can a man take fire in his bosom and his clothes not be burned?

²⁸Can one go upon hot coals and his feet not be burned?

²⁹So he who cohabits with his neighbor's wife [will be tortured with evil consequences and just retribution]; he who touches her shall not be innocent or go unpunished.

[30]Men do not despise a thief if he steals to satisfy himself when he is hungry;

[31]But if he is found out, he must restore seven times [what he stole]; he must give the whole substance of his house [if necessary--to meet his fine].

[32]But whoever commits adultery with a woman lacks heart and understanding (moral principle and prudence); he who does it is destroying his own life.

[33]Wounds and disgrace will he get, and his reproach will not be wiped away.

[34]For jealousy makes [the wronged] man furious; therefore he will not spare in the day of vengeance [upon the detected one].

[35]He will not consider any ransom [offered to buy him off from demanding full punishment]; neither will he be satisfied, though you offer him many gifts and bribes.

PROVERBS 7

[1]MY SON, keep my words; lay up within you my commandments [for use when needed] and treasure them.

[2]Keep my commandments and live, and keep my law and teaching as the apple (the pupil) of your eye.

[3]Bind them on your fingers; write them on the tablet of your heart.

[4]Say to skillful and godly Wisdom, You are my sister, and regard understanding or insight as your intimate friend--

[5]That they may keep you from the loose woman, from the adventuress who flatters with and makes smooth her words.

[6]For at the window of my house I looked out through my lattice.

[7]And among the simple (empty-headed and emptyhearted) ones, I perceived among the youths a young man void of good sense,

[8]Sauntering through the street near the [loose woman's] corner; and he went the way to her house

[9]In the twilight, in the evening; night black and dense was falling [over the young man's life].

[10]And behold, there met him a woman, dressed as a harlot and sly and cunning of heart.

[11]She is turbulent and willful; her feet stay not in her house;

[12]Now in the streets, now in the marketplaces, she sets her ambush at every corner.

¹³So she caught him and kissed him and with impudent face she said to him,

¹⁴Sacrifices of peace offerings were due from me; this day I paid my vows.

¹⁵So I came forth to meet you [that you might share with me the feast from my offering]; diligently I sought your face, and I have found you.

¹⁶I have spread my couch with rugs and cushions of tapestry, with striped sheets of fine linen of Egypt.

¹⁷I have perfumed my bed with myrrh, aloes, and cinnamon.

¹⁸Come, let us take our fill of love until morning; let us console and delight ourselves with love.

¹⁹For the man is not at home; he is gone on a long journey;

²⁰He has taken a bag of money with him and will come home at the day appointed [at the full moon].

²¹With much justifying and enticing argument she persuades him, with the allurements of her lips she leads him [to overcome his conscience and his fears] and forces him along.

²²Suddenly he [yields and] follows her reluctantly like an ox moving to the slaughter, like one in fetters going to the correction [to be given] to a fool or like a dog enticed by food to the muzzle

²³Till a dart [of passion] pierces and inflames his vitals; then like a bird fluttering straight into the net [he hastens], not knowing that it will cost him his life.

²⁴Listen to me now therefore, O you sons, and be attentive to the words of my mouth.

²⁵Let not your heart incline toward her ways, do not stray into her paths.

²⁶For she has cast down many wounded; indeed, all her slain are a mighty host.

²⁷Her house is the way to Sheol (Hades, the place of the dead), going down to the chambers of death.

PROVERBS 8

¹DOES NOT skillful and godly Wisdom cry out, and understanding raise her voice [in contrast to the loose woman]?

²On the top of the heights beside the way, where the paths meet, stands Wisdom [skillful and godly];

³At the gates at the entrance of the town, at the coming in at the doors, she cries out:

⁴To you, O men, I call, and my voice is directed to the sons of men.

⁵O you simple and thoughtless ones, understand prudence; you [self-confident] fools, be of an understanding heart.

⁶Hear, for I will speak excellent and princely things; and the opening of my lips shall be for right things.

⁷For my mouth shall utter truth, and wrongdoing is detestable and loathsome to my lips.

⁸All the words of my mouth are righteous (upright and in right standing with God); there is nothing contrary to truth or crooked in them.

⁹They are all plain to him who understands [and opens his heart], and right to those who find knowledge [and live by it].

¹⁰Receive my instruction in preference to [striving for] silver, and knowledge rather than choice gold,

¹¹For skillful and godly Wisdom is better than rubies or pearls, and all the things that may be desired are not to be compared to it.

¹²I, Wisdom [from God], make prudence my dwelling, and I find out knowledge and discretion.

¹³The reverent fear and worshipful awe of the Lord [includes] the hatred of evil; pride, arrogance, the evil way, and perverted and twisted speech I hate.

¹⁴I have counsel and sound knowledge, I have understanding, I have might and power.

¹⁵By me kings reign and rulers decree justice.

¹⁶By me princes rule, and nobles, even all the judges and governors of the earth.

¹⁷I love those who love me, and those who seek me early and diligently shall find me.

¹⁸Riches and honor are with me, enduring wealth and righteousness (uprightness in every area and relation, and right standing with God).

¹⁹My fruit is better than gold, yes, than refined gold, and my increase than choice silver.

²⁰I [Wisdom] walk in the way of righteousness (moral and spiritual rectitude in every area and relation), in the midst of the paths of justice,

²¹That I may cause those who love me to inherit [true] riches and that I may fill their treasuries.

²²The Lord formed and brought me [Wisdom] forth at the beginning of His way, before His acts of old.

²³I [Wisdom] was inaugurated and ordained from everlasting, from the beginning, before ever the earth existed.

²⁴When there were no deeps, I was brought forth, when there were no fountains laden with water.

²⁵Before the mountains were settled, before the hills, I was brought forth,

²⁶While as yet He had not made the land or the fields or the first of the dust of the earth.

²⁷When He prepared the heavens, I [Wisdom] was there; when He drew a circle upon the face of the deep and stretched out the firmament over it,

²⁸When He made firm the skies above, when He established the fountains of the deep,

²⁹When He gave to the sea its limit and His decree that the waters should not transgress [across the boundaries set by] His command, when He appointed the foundations of the earth--

³⁰Then I [Wisdom] was beside Him as a master and director of the work; and I was daily His delight, rejoicing before Him always,

³¹Rejoicing in His inhabited earth and delighting in the sons of men.

³²Now therefore listen to me, O you sons; for blessed (happy, fortunate, to be envied) are those who keep my ways.

³³Hear instruction and be wise, and do not refuse or neglect it.

³⁴Blessed (happy, fortunate, to be envied) is the man who listens to me, watching daily at my gates, waiting at the posts of my doors.

³⁵For whoever finds me [Wisdom] finds life and draws forth and obtains favor from the Lord.

³⁶But he who misses me or sins against me wrongs and injures himself; all who hate me love and court death.

PROVERBS 9

¹WISDOM HAS built her house; she has hewn out and set up her seven [perfect number of] pillars.

²She has killed her beasts, she has mixed her [spiritual] wine; she has also set her table.

³She has sent out her maids to cry from the highest places of the town:

⁴Whoever is simple (easily led astray and wavering), let him turn in here! As for him who lacks understanding, [God's] Wisdom says to him,

⁵Come, eat of my bread and drink of the [spiritual] wine which I have mixed.

⁶Leave off, simple ones [forsake the foolish and simpleminded] and live! And walk in the way of insight and understanding.

⁷He who rebukes a scorner heaps upon himself abuse, and he who reproves a wicked man gets for himself bruises.

⁸Reprove not a scorner, lest he hate you; reprove a wise man, and he will love you.

⁹Give instruction to a wise man and he will be yet wiser; teach a righteous man (one upright and in right standing with God) and he will increase in learning.

¹⁰The reverent and worshipful fear of the Lord is the beginning (the chief and choice part) of Wisdom, and the knowledge of the Holy One is insight and understanding.

¹¹For by me [Wisdom from God] your days shall be multiplied, and the years of your life shall be increased.

¹²If you are wise, you are wise for yourself; if you scorn, you alone will bear it and pay the penalty.

¹³The foolish woman is noisy; she is simple and open to all forms of evil, she [willfully and recklessly] knows nothing whatever [of eternal value].

¹⁴For she sits at the door of her house or on a seat in the conspicuous places of the town,

¹⁵Calling to those who pass by, who go uprightly on their way:

¹⁶Whoever is simple (wavering and easily led astray), let him turn in here! And as for him who lacks understanding, she says to him,

¹⁷Stolen waters (pleasures) are sweet [because they are forbidden]; and bread eaten in secret is pleasant.

¹⁸But he knows not that the shades of the dead are there [specters haunting the scene of past transgressions], and that her invited guests are [already sunk] in the depths of Sheol (the lower world, Hades, the place of the dead).

PROVERBS 10

¹THE PROVERBS of Solomon: A wise son makes a glad father, but a foolish and self-confident son is the grief of his mother.

²Treasures of wickedness profit nothing, but righteousness (moral and spiritual rectitude in every area and relation) delivers from death.

³The Lord will not allow the [uncompromisingly] righteous to famish, but He thwarts the desire of the wicked.

⁴He becomes poor who works with a slack and idle hand, but the hand of the diligent makes rich.

⁵He who gathers in summer is a wise son, but he who sleeps in harvest is a son who causes shame.

⁶Blessings are upon the head of the [uncompromisingly] righteous (the upright, in right standing with God) but the mouth of the wicked conceals violence.

⁷The memory of the [uncompromisingly] righteous is a blessing, but the name of the wicked shall rot.

⁸The wise in heart will accept and obey commandments, but the foolish of lips will fall headlong.

⁹He who walks uprightly walks securely, but he who takes a crooked way shall be found out and punished.

¹⁰He who winks with the eye [craftily and with malice] causes sorrow; the foolish of lips will fall headlong but he who boldly reproves makes peace.

¹¹The mouth of the [uncompromisingly] righteous man is a well of life, but the mouth of the wicked conceals violence.

¹²Hatred stirs up contentions, but love covers all transgressions.

¹³On the lips of him who has discernment skillful and godly Wisdom is found, but discipline and the rod are for the back of him who is without sense and understanding.

¹⁴Wise men store up knowledge [in mind and heart], but the mouth of the foolish is a present destruction.

¹⁵The rich man's wealth is his strong city; the poverty of the poor is their ruin.

¹⁶The earnings of the righteous (the upright, in right standing with God) lead to life, but the profit of the wicked leads to further sin.

[17]He who heeds instruction and correction is [not only himself] in the way of life [but also] is a way of life for others. And he who neglects or refuses reproof [not only himself] goes astray [but also] causes to err and is a path toward ruin for others.

[18]He who hides hatred is of lying lips, and he who utters slander is a [self-confident] fool.

[19]In a multitude of words transgression is not lacking, but he who restrains his lips is prudent.

[20]The tongues of those who are upright and in right standing with God are as choice silver; the minds of those who are wicked and out of harmony with God are of little value.

[21]The lips of the [uncompromisingly] righteous feed and guide many, but fools die for want of understanding and heart.

[22]The blessing of the Lord--it makes [truly] rich, and He adds no sorrow with it [neither does toiling increase it].

[23]It is as sport to a [self-confident] fool to do wickedness, but to have skillful and godly Wisdom is pleasure and relaxation to a man of understanding.

[24]The thing a wicked man fears shall come upon him, but the desire of the [uncompromisingly] righteous shall be granted.

[25]When the whirlwind passes, the wicked are no more, but the [uncompromisingly] righteous have an everlasting foundation.

[26]As vinegar to the teeth and as smoke to the eyes, so is the sluggard to those who employ and send him.

[27]The reverent and worshipful fear of the Lord prolongs one's days, but the years of the wicked shall be made short.

[28]The hope of the [uncompromisingly] righteous (the upright, in right standing with God) is gladness, but the expectation of the wicked (those who are out of harmony with God) comes to nothing.

[29]The way of the Lord is strength and a stronghold to the upright, but it is destruction to the workers of iniquity.

[30]The [consistently] righteous shall never be removed, but the wicked shall not inhabit the earth [eventually].

[31]The mouths of the righteous (those harmonious with God) bring forth skillful and godly Wisdom, but the perverse tongue shall be cut down [like a barren and rotten tree].

³²The lips of the [uncompromisingly] righteous know [and therefore utter] what is acceptable, but the mouth of the wicked knows [and therefore speaks only] what is obstinately willful and contrary.

PROVERBS 11

¹A FALSE balance and unrighteous dealings are extremely offensive and shamefully sinful to the Lord, but a just weight is His delight.

²When swelling and pride come, then emptiness and shame come also, but with the humble (those who are lowly, who have been pruned or chiseled by trial, and renounce self) are skillful and godly Wisdom and soundness.

³The integrity of the upright shall guide them, but the willful contrariness and crookedness of the treacherous shall destroy them.

⁴Riches provide no security in any day of wrath and judgment, but righteousness (uprightness and right standing with God) delivers from death.

⁵The righteousness of the blameless shall rectify and make plain their way and keep it straight, but the wicked shall fall by their own wickedness.

⁶The righteousness of the upright [their rectitude in every area and relation] shall deliver them, but the treacherous shall be taken in their own iniquity and greedy desire.

⁷When the wicked man dies, his hope [for the future] perishes; and the expectation of the godless comes to nothing.

⁸The [uncompromisingly] righteous is delivered out of trouble, and the wicked gets into it instead.

⁹With his mouth the godless man destroys his neighbor, but through knowledge and superior discernment shall the righteous be delivered.

¹⁰When it goes well with the [uncompromisingly] righteous, the city rejoices, but when the wicked perish, there are shouts of joy.

¹¹By the blessing of the influence of the upright and God's favor [because of them] the city is exalted, but it is overthrown by the mouth of the wicked.

¹²He who belittles and despises his neighbor lacks sense, but a man of understanding keeps silent.

¹³He who goes about as a talebearer reveals secrets, but he who is trustworthy and faithful in spirit keeps the matter hidden.

¹⁴Where no wise guidance is, the people fall, but in the multitude of counselors there is safety.

¹⁵He who becomes security for an outsider shall smart for it, but he who hates suretyship is secure [from its penalties].

¹⁶A gracious and good woman wins honor [for her husband], and violent men win riches but a woman who hates righteousness is a throne of dishonor for him.

¹⁷The merciful, kind, and generous man benefits himself [for his deeds return to bless him], but he who is cruel and callous [to the wants of others] brings on himself retribution.

¹⁸The wicked man earns deceitful wages, but he who sows righteousness (moral and spiritual rectitude in every area and relation) shall have a sure reward [permanent and satisfying].

¹⁹He who is steadfast in righteousness (uprightness and right standing with God) attains to life, but he who pursues evil does it to his own death.

²⁰They who are willfully contrary in heart are extremely disgusting and shamefully vile in the eyes of the Lord, but such as are blameless and wholehearted in their ways are His delight!

²¹Assuredly [I pledge it] the wicked shall not go unpunished, but the multitude of the [uncompromisingly] righteous shall be delivered.

²²As a ring of gold in a swine's snout, so is a fair woman who is without discretion.

²³The desire of the righteous brings only good, but the expectation of the wicked brings wrath.

²⁴There are those who [generously] scatter abroad, and yet increase more; there are those who withhold more than is fitting or what is justly due, but it results only in want.

²⁵The liberal person shall be enriched, and he who waters shall himself be watered.

²⁶The people curse him who holds back grain [when the public needs it], but a blessing [from God and man] is upon the head of him who sells it.

²⁷He who diligently seeks good seeks [God's] favor, but he who searches after evil, it shall come upon him.

²⁸He who leans on, trusts in, and is confident in his riches shall fall, but the [uncompromisingly] righteous shall flourish like a green bough.

²⁹He who troubles his own house shall inherit the wind, and the foolish shall be servant to the wise of heart.

³⁰The fruit of the [uncompromisingly] righteous is a tree of life, and he who is wise captures human lives [for God, as a fisher of men--he gathers and receives them for eternity].

³¹Behold, the [uncompromisingly] righteous shall be recompensed on earth; how much more the wicked and the sinner! And if the righteous are barely saved, what will become of the ungodly and wicked?

PROVERBS 12

¹WHOEVER LOVES instruction and correction loves knowledge, but he who hates reproof is like a brute beast, stupid and indiscriminating.

²A good man obtains favor from the Lord, but a man of wicked devices He condemns.

³A man shall not be established by wickedness, but the root of the [uncompromisingly] righteous shall never be moved.

⁴A virtuous and worthy wife [earnest and strong in character] is a crowning joy to her husband, but she who makes him ashamed is as rottenness in his bones.

⁵The thoughts and purposes of the [consistently] righteous are honest and reliable, but the counsels and designs of the wicked are treacherous.

⁶The words of the wicked lie in wait for blood, but the mouth of the upright shall deliver them and the innocent ones [thus endangered].

⁷The wicked are overthrown and are not, but the house of the [uncompromisingly] righteous shall stand.

⁸A man shall be commended according to his Wisdom [godly Wisdom, which is comprehensive insight into the ways and purposes of God], but he who is of a perverse heart shall be despised.

⁹Better is he who is lightly esteemed but works for his own support than he who assumes honor for himself and lacks bread.

¹⁰A [consistently] righteous man regards the life of his beast, but even the tender mercies of the wicked are cruel.

¹¹He who tills his land shall be satisfied with bread, but he who follows worthless pursuits is lacking in sense and is without understanding.

¹²The wicked desire the booty of evil men, but the root of the [uncompromisingly] righteous yields [richer fruitage].

¹³The wicked is [dangerously] snared by the transgression of his lips, but the [uncompromisingly] righteous shall come out of trouble.

¹⁴From the fruit of his words a man shall be satisfied with good, and the work of a man's hands shall come back to him [as a harvest].

¹⁵The way of a fool is right in his own eyes, but he who listens to counsel is wise.

¹⁶A fool's wrath is quickly and openly known, but a prudent man ignores an insult.

¹⁷He who breathes out truth shows forth righteousness (uprightness and right standing with God), but a false witness utters deceit.

¹⁸There are those who speak rashly, like the piercing of a sword, but the tongue of the wise brings healing.

¹⁹Truthful lips shall be established forever, but a lying tongue is [credited] but for a moment.

²⁰Deceit is in the hearts of those who devise evil, but for the counselors of peace there is joy.

²¹No [actual] evil, misfortune, or calamity shall come upon the righteous, but the wicked shall be filled with evil, misfortune, and calamity.

²²Lying lips are extremely disgusting and hateful to the Lord, but they who deal faithfully are His delight.

²³A prudent man is reluctant to display his knowledge, but the heart of [self-confident] fools proclaims their folly.

²⁴The hand of the diligent will rule, but the slothful will be put to forced labor.

²⁵Anxiety in a man's heart weighs it down, but an encouraging word makes it glad.

²⁶The [consistently] righteous man is a guide to his neighbor, but the way of the wicked causes others to go astray.

²⁷The slothful man does not catch his game or roast it once he kills it, but the diligent man gets precious possessions.

²⁸Life is in the way of righteousness (moral and spiritual rectitude in every area and relation), and in its pathway there is no death but immortality (perpetual, eternal life).

PROVERBS 13

¹A WISE son heeds [and is the fruit of] his father's instruction and correction, but a scoffer listens not to rebuke.

²A good man eats good from the fruit of his mouth, but the desire of the treacherous is for violence.

³He who guards his mouth keeps his life, but he who opens wide his lips comes to ruin.

⁴The appetite of the sluggard craves and gets nothing, but the appetite of the diligent is abundantly supplied.

⁵A [consistently] righteous man hates lying and deceit, but a wicked man is loathsome [his very breath spreads pollution] and he comes [surely] to shame.

⁶Righteousness (rightness and justice in every area and relation) guards him who is upright in the way, but wickedness plunges into sin and overthrows the sinner.

⁷One man considers himself rich, yet has nothing [to keep permanently]; another man considers himself poor, yet has great [and indestructible] riches.

⁸A rich man can buy his way out of threatened death by paying a ransom, but the poor man does not even have to listen to threats [from the envious].

⁹The light of the [uncompromisingly] righteous [is within him--it grows brighter and] rejoices, but the lamp of the wicked [furnishes only a derived, temporary light and] shall be put out shortly.

¹⁰By pride and insolence comes only contention, but with the well-advised is skillful and godly Wisdom.

¹¹Wealth [not earned but] won in haste or unjustly or from the production of things for vain or detrimental use [such riches] will dwindle away, but he who gathers little by little will increase [his riches].

¹²Hope deferred makes the heart sick, but when the desire is fulfilled, it is a tree of life.

¹³Whoever despises the word and counsel [of God] brings destruction upon himself, but he who [reverently] fears and respects the commandment [of God] is rewarded.

¹⁴The teaching of the wise is a fountain of life, that one may avoid the snares of death.

¹⁵Good understanding wins favor, but the way of the transgressor is hard [like the barren, dry soil or the impassable swamp].

¹⁶Every prudent man deals with knowledge, but a [self-confident] fool exposes and flaunts his folly.

¹⁷A wicked messenger falls into evil, but a faithful ambassador brings healing.

¹⁸Poverty and shame come to him who refuses instruction and correction, but he who heeds reproof is honored.

¹⁹Satisfied desire is sweet to a person; therefore it is hateful and exceedingly offensive to [self-confident] fools to give up evil [upon which they have set their hearts].

²⁰He who walks [as a companion] with wise men is wise, but he who associates with [self-confident] fools is [a fool himself and] shall smart for it.

²¹Evil pursues sinners, but the consistently upright and in right standing with God is recompensed with good.

²²A good man leaves an inheritance [of moral stability and goodness] to his children's children, and the wealth of the sinner [finds its way eventually] into the hands of the righteous, for whom it was laid up.

²³Much food is in the tilled land of the poor, but there are those who are destroyed because of injustice.

²⁴He who spares his rod [of discipline] hates his son, but he who loves him disciplines diligently and punishes him early.

²⁵The [uncompromisingly] righteous eats to his own satisfaction, but the stomach of the wicked is in want.

PROVERBS 14

¹EVERY WISE woman builds her house, but the foolish one tears it down with her own hands.

²He who walks in uprightness reverently and worshipfully fears the Lord, but he who is contrary and devious in his ways despises Him.

³In the [a]fool's own mouth is a rod [to shame] his pride, but the wise men's lips preserve them.

⁴Where no oxen are, the grain crib is empty, but much increase [of crops] comes by the strength of the ox.

⁵A faithful witness will not lie, but a false witness breathes out falsehoods.

⁶A scoffer seeks Wisdom in vain [for his very attitude blinds and deafens him to it], but knowledge is easy to him who [being teachable] understands.

⁷Go from the presence of a foolish and self-confident man, for you will not find knowledge on his lips.

⁸The Wisdom [godly Wisdom, which is comprehensive insight into the ways and purposes of God] of the prudent is to understand his way, but the folly of [self-confident] fools is to deceive.

⁹Fools make a mock of sin and sin mocks the fools [who are its victims; a sin offering made by them only mocks them, bringing them disappointment and disfavor], but among the upright there is the favor of God.

¹⁰The heart knows its own bitterness, and no stranger shares its joy.

¹¹The house of the wicked shall be overthrown, but the tent of the upright shall flourish.

¹²There is a way which seems right to a man and appears straight before him, but at the end of it is the way of death.

¹³Even in laughter the heart is sorrowful, and the end of mirth is heaviness and grief.

¹⁴The backslider in heart [from God and from fearing God] shall be filled with [the fruit of] his own ways, and a good man shall be satisfied with [the fruit of] his ways [with the holy thoughts and actions which his heart prompts and in which he delights].

¹⁵The simpleton believes every word he hears, but the prudent man looks and considers well where he is going.

¹⁶A wise man suspects danger and cautiously avoids evil, but the fool bears himself insolently and is [presumptuously] confident.

¹⁷He who foams up quickly and flies into a passion deals foolishly, and a man of wicked plots and plans is hated.

¹⁸The simple acquire folly, but the prudent are crowned with knowledge.

¹⁹The evil men bow before the good, and the wicked [stand suppliantly] at the gates of the [uncompromisingly] righteous.

²⁰The poor is hated even by his own neighbor, but the rich has many friends.

²¹He who despises his neighbor sins [against God, his fellowman, and himself], but happy (blessed and fortunate) is he who is kind and merciful to the poor.

²²Do they not err who devise evil and wander from the way of life? But loving-kindness and mercy, loyalty and faithfulness, shall be to those who devise good.

²³In all labor there is profit, but idle talk leads only to poverty.

²⁴The crown of the wise is their wealth of Wisdom, but the foolishness of [self-confident] fools is [nothing but] folly.

²⁵A truthful witness saves lives, but a deceitful witness speaks lies [and endangers lives].

²⁶In the reverent and worshipful fear of the Lord there is strong confidence, and His children shall always have a place of refuge.

²⁷Reverent and worshipful fear of the Lord is a fountain of life, that one may avoid the snares of death.

²⁸In a multitude of people is the king's glory, but in a lack of people is the prince's ruin.

²⁹He who is slow to anger has great understanding, but he who is hasty of spirit exposes and exalts his folly.

³⁰A calm and undisturbed mind and heart are the life and health of the body, but envy, jealousy, and wrath are like rottenness of the bones.

³¹He who oppresses the poor reproaches, mocks, and insults his Maker, but he who is kind and merciful to the needy honors Him.

³²The wicked is overthrown through his wrongdoing and calamity, but the [consistently] righteous has hope and confidence even in death.

³³Wisdom rests [silently] in the mind and heart of him who has understanding, but that which is in the inward part of [self-confident] fools is made known.

³⁴Uprightness and right standing with God (moral and spiritual rectitude in every area and relation) elevate a nation, but sin is a reproach to any people.

³⁵The king's favor is toward a wise and discreet servant, but his wrath is against him who does shamefully.

PROVERBS 15

¹A SOFT answer turns away wrath, but grievous words stir up anger.

²The tongue of the wise utters knowledge rightly, but the mouth of the [self-confident] fool pours out folly.

³The eyes of the Lord are in every place, keeping watch upon the evil and the good.

⁴A gentle tongue [with its healing power] is a tree of life, but willful contrariness in it breaks down the spirit.

⁵A fool despises his father's instruction and correction, but he who regards reproof acquires prudence.

⁶In the house of the [uncompromisingly] righteous is great [priceless] treasure, but with the income of the wicked is trouble and vexation.

⁷The lips of the wise disperse knowledge [sifting it as chaff from the grain]; not so the minds and hearts of the self-confident and foolish.

⁸The sacrifice of the wicked is an abomination, hateful and exceedingly offensive to the Lord, but the prayer of the upright is His delight!

⁹The way of the wicked is an abomination, extremely disgusting and shamefully vile to the Lord, but He loves him who pursues righteousness (moral and spiritual rectitude in every area and relation).

¹⁰There is severe discipline for him who forsakes God's way; and he who hates reproof will die [physically, morally, and spiritually].

¹¹Sheol (the place of the dead) and Abaddon (the abyss, the final place of the accuser Satan) are both before the Lord--how much more, then, the hearts of the children of men?

¹²A scorner has no love for one who rebukes him; neither will he go to the wise [for counsel].

¹³A glad heart makes a cheerful countenance, but by sorrow of heart the spirit is broken.

¹⁴The mind of him who has understanding seeks knowledge and inquires after and craves it, but the mouth of the [self-confident] fool feeds on folly.

¹⁵All the days of the desponding and afflicted are made evil [by anxious thoughts and forebodings], but he who has a glad heart has a continual feast [regardless of circumstances].

¹⁶Better is little with the reverent, worshipful fear of the Lord than great and rich treasure and trouble with it.

¹⁷Better is a dinner of herbs where love is than a fatted ox and hatred with it.

¹⁸A hot-tempered man stirs up strife, but he who is slow to anger appeases contention.

¹⁹The way of the sluggard is overgrown with thorns [it pricks, lacerates, and entangles him], but the way of the righteous is plain and raised like a highway.

²⁰A wise son makes a glad father, but a self-confident and foolish man despises his mother and puts her to shame.

²¹Folly is pleasure to him who is without heart and sense, but a man of understanding walks uprightly [making straight his course].

²²Where there is no counsel, purposes are frustrated, but with many counselors they are accomplished.

²³A man has joy in making an apt answer, and a word spoken at the right moment--how good it is!

²⁴The path of the wise leads upward to life, that he may avoid [the gloom] in the depths of Sheol (Hades, the place of the dead).

²⁵The Lord tears down the house of the proud, but He makes secure the boundaries of the [consecrated] widow.

²⁶The thoughts of the wicked are shamefully vile and exceedingly offensive to the Lord, but the words of the pure are pleasing words to Him.

²⁷He who is greedy for unjust gain troubles his own household, but he who hates bribes will live.

²⁸The mind of the [uncompromisingly] righteous studies how to answer, but the mouth of the wicked pours out evil things.

²⁹The Lord is far from the wicked, but He hears the prayer of the [consistently] righteous (the upright, in right standing with Him).

³⁰The light in the eyes [of him whose heart is joyful] rejoices the hearts of others, and good news nourishes the bones.

³¹The ear that listens to the reproof [that leads to or gives] life will remain among the wise.

³²He who refuses and ignores instruction and correction despises himself, but he who heeds reproof gets understanding.

³³The reverent and worshipful fear of the Lord brings instruction in Wisdom, and humility comes before honor.

PROVERBS 16

¹THE PLANS of the mind and orderly thinking belong to man, but from the Lord comes the [wise] answer of the tongue.

²All the ways of a man are pure in his own eyes, but the Lord weighs the spirits (the thoughts and intents of the heart).

³Roll your works upon the Lord [commit and trust them wholly to Him; He will cause your thoughts to become agreeable to His will, and] so shall your plans be established and succeed.

⁴The Lord has made everything [to accommodate itself and contribute] to its own end and His own purpose--even the wicked [are fitted for their role] for the day of calamity and evil.

⁵Everyone proud and arrogant in heart is disgusting, hateful, and exceedingly offensive to the Lord; be assured [I pledge it] they will not go unpunished.

⁶By mercy and love, truth and fidelity [to God and man--not by sacrificial offerings], iniquity is purged out of the heart, and by the reverent, worshipful fear of the Lord men depart from and avoid evil.

⁷When a man's ways please the Lord, He makes even his enemies to be at peace with him.

⁸Better is a little with righteousness (uprightness in every area and relation and right standing with God) than great revenues with injustice.

⁹A man's mind plans his way, but the Lord directs his steps and makes them sure.

¹⁰Divinely directed decisions are on the lips of the king; his mouth should not transgress in judgment.

¹¹A just balance and scales are the Lord's; all the weights of the bag are His work [established on His eternal principles].

¹²It is an abomination [to God and men] for kings to commit wickedness, for a throne is established and made secure by righteousness (moral and spiritual rectitude in every area and relation).

¹³Right and just lips are the delight of a king, and he loves him who speaks what is right.

¹⁴The wrath of a king is as messengers of death, but a wise man will pacify it.

¹⁵In the light of the king's countenance is life, and his favor is as a cloud bringing the spring rain.

¹⁶How much better it is to get skillful and godly Wisdom than gold! And to get understanding is to be chosen rather than silver.

¹⁷The highway of the upright turns aside from evil; he who guards his way preserves his life.

¹⁸Pride goes before destruction, and a haughty spirit before a fall.

¹⁹Better it is to be of a humble spirit with the meek and poor than to divide the spoil with the proud.

²⁰He who deals wisely and heeds [God's] word and counsel shall find good, and whoever leans on, trusts in, and is confident in the Lord--happy, blessed, and fortunate is he.

²¹The wise in heart are called prudent, understanding, and knowing, and winsome speech increases learning [in both speaker and listener].

²²Understanding is a wellspring of life to those who have it, but to give instruction to fools is folly.

²³The mind of the wise instructs his mouth, and adds learning and persuasiveness to his lips.

²⁴Pleasant words are as a honeycomb, sweet to the mind and healing to the body.

²⁵There is a way that seems right to a man and appears straight before him, but at the end of it is the way of death.

²⁶The appetite of the laborer works for him, for [the need of] his mouth urges him on.

²⁷A worthless man devises and digs up mischief, and in his lips there is as a scorching fire.

²⁸A perverse man sows strife, and a whisperer separates close friends.

²⁹The exceedingly grasping, covetous, and violent man entices his neighbor, leading him in a way that is not good.

³⁰He who shuts his eyes to devise perverse things and who compresses his lips [as if in concealment] brings evil to pass.

³¹The hoary head is a crown of beauty and glory if it is found in the way of righteousness (moral and spiritual rectitude in every area and relation).

³²He who is slow to anger is better than the mighty, he who rules his [own] spirit than he who takes a city.

³³The lot is cast into the lap, but the decision is wholly of the Lord [even the events that seem accidental are really ordered by Him].

PROVERBS 17

¹BETTER IS a dry morsel with quietness than a house full of feasting [on offered sacrifices] with strife.

²A wise servant shall have rule over a son who causes shame, and shall share in the inheritance among the brothers.

³The refining pot is for silver and the furnace for gold, but the Lord tries the hearts.

⁴An evildoer gives heed to wicked lips; and a liar listens to a mischievous tongue.

⁵Whoever mocks the poor reproaches his Maker, and he who is glad at calamity shall not be held innocent or go unpunished.

⁶Children's children are the crown of old men, and the glory of children is their fathers.

⁷Fine or arrogant speech does not befit [an empty-headed] fool-- much less do lying lips befit a prince.

⁸A bribe is like a bright, precious stone that dazzles the eyes and affects the mind of him who gives it; [as if by magic] he prospers, whichever way he turns.

⁹He who covers and forgives an offense seeks love, but he who repeats or harps on a matter separates even close friends.

¹⁰A reproof enters deeper into a man of understanding than a hundred lashes into a [self-confident] fool.

¹¹An evil man seeks only rebellion; therefore a stern and pitiless messenger shall be sent against him.

¹²Let [the brute ferocity of] a bear robbed of her whelps meet a man rather than a [self-confident] fool in his folly [when he is in a rage].

¹³Whoever rewards evil for good, evil shall not depart from his house.

¹⁴The beginning of strife is as when water first trickles [from a crack in a dam]; therefore stop contention before it becomes worse and quarreling breaks out.

¹⁵He who justifies the wicked and he who condemns the righteous are both an abomination [exceedingly disgusting and hateful] to the Lord.

¹⁶Of what use is money in the hand of a [self-confident] fool to buy skillful and godly Wisdom--when he has no understanding or heart for it?

¹⁷A friend loves at all times, and is born, as is a brother, for adversity.

¹⁸A man void of good sense gives a pledge and becomes security for another in the presence of his neighbor.

¹⁹He who loves strife and is quarrelsome loves transgression and involves himself in guilt; he who raises high his gateway and is boastful and arrogant invites destruction.

²⁰He who has a wayward and crooked mind finds no good, and he who has a willful and contrary tongue will fall into calamity.

²¹He who becomes the parent of a [self-confident] fool does it to his sorrow, and the father of [an empty-headed] fool has no joy [in him].

²²A happy heart is good medicine and a cheerful mind works healing, but a broken spirit dries up the bones.

²³A wicked man receives a bribe out of the bosom (pocket) to pervert the ways of justice.

²⁴A man of understanding sets skillful and godly Wisdom before his face, but the eyes of a [self-confident] fool are on the ends of the earth.

²⁵A self-confident and foolish son is a grief to his father and bitterness to her who bore him.

²⁶Also, to punish or fine the righteous is not good, nor to smite the noble for their uprightness.

²⁷He who has knowledge spares his words, and a man of understanding has a cool spirit.

²⁸Even a fool when he holds his peace is considered wise; when he closes his lips he is esteemed a man of understanding.

PROVERBS 18

¹HE WHO willfully separates and estranges himself [from God and man] seeks his own desire and pretext to break out against all wise and sound judgment.

²A [self-confident] fool has no delight in understanding but only in revealing his personal opinions and himself.

³When the wicked comes in [to the depth of evil], he becomes a contemptuous despiser [of all that is pure and good], and with inner baseness comes outer shame and reproach.

⁴The words of a [discreet and wise] man's mouth are like deep waters [plenteous and difficult to fathom], and the fountain of skillful and godly Wisdom is like a gushing stream [sparkling, fresh, pure, and life-giving].

⁵To respect the person of the wicked and be partial to him, so as to deprive the [consistently] righteous of justice, is not good.

⁶A [self-confident] fool's lips bring contention, and his mouth invites a beating.

⁷A [self-confident] fool's mouth is his ruin, and his lips are a snare to himself.

⁸The words of a whisperer or talebearer are as dainty morsels; they go down into the innermost parts of the body.

⁹He who is loose and slack in his work is brother to him who is a destroyer and he who does not use his endeavors to heal himself is brother to him who commits suicide.

¹⁰The name of the Lord is a strong tower; the [consistently] righteous man [upright and in right standing with God] runs into it and is safe, high [above evil] and strong.

¹¹The rich man's wealth is his strong city, and as a high protecting wall in his own imagination and conceit.

¹²Haughtiness comes before disaster, but humility before honor.

¹³He who answers a matter before he hears the facts--it is folly and shame to him.

¹⁴The strong spirit of a man sustains him in bodily pain or trouble, but a weak and broken spirit who can raise up or bear?

¹⁵The mind of the prudent is ever getting knowledge, and the ear of the wise is ever seeking (inquiring for and craving) knowledge.

¹⁶A man's gift makes room for him and brings him before great men.

¹⁷He who states his case first seems right, until his rival comes and cross-examines him.

¹⁸To cast lots puts an end to disputes and decides between powerful contenders.

¹⁹A brother offended is harder to be won over than a strong city, and [their] contentions separate them like the bars of a castle.

²⁰A man's [moral] self shall be filled with the fruit of his mouth; and with the consequence of his words he must be satisfied [whether good or evil].

²¹Death and life are in the power of the tongue, and they who indulge in it shall eat the fruit of it [for death or life].

²²He who finds a [true] wife finds a good thing and obtains favor from the Lord.

²³The poor man uses entreaties, but the rich answers roughly.

²⁴The man of many friends [a friend of all the world] will prove himself a bad friend, but there is a friend who sticks closer than a brother.

PROVERBS 19

¹BETTER IS a poor man who walks in his integrity than a rich man who is perverse in his speech and is a [self-confident] fool.

²Desire without knowledge is not good, and to be overhasty is to sin and miss the mark.

³The foolishness of man subverts his way [ruins his affairs]; then his heart is resentful and frets against the Lord.

⁴Wealth makes many friends, but the poor man is avoided by his neighbor.

⁵A false witness shall not be unpunished, and he who breathes out lies shall not escape.

⁶Many will entreat the favor of a liberal man, and every man is a friend to him who gives gifts.

⁷All the brothers of a poor man detest him--how much more do his friends go far from him! He pursues them with words, but they are gone.

⁸He who gains Wisdom loves his own life; he who keeps understanding shall prosper and find good.

⁹A false witness shall not be unpunished, and he who breathes forth lies shall perish.

¹⁰Luxury is not fitting for a [self-confident] fool--much less for a slave to rule over princes.

¹¹Good sense makes a man restrain his anger, and it is his glory to overlook a transgression or an offense.

¹²The king's wrath is as terrifying as the roaring of a lion, but his favor is as [refreshing as] dew upon the grass.

¹³A self-confident and foolish son is the [multiplied] calamity of his father, and the contentions of a wife are like a continual dripping [of water through a chink in the roof].

¹⁴House and riches are the inheritance from fathers, but a wise, understanding, and prudent wife is from the Lord.

¹⁵Slothfulness casts one into a deep sleep, and the idle person shall suffer hunger.

¹⁶He who keeps the commandment [of the Lord] keeps his own life, but he who despises His ways shall die.

¹⁷He who has pity on the poor lends to the Lord, and that which he has given He will repay to him.

¹⁸Discipline your son while there is hope, but do not [indulge your angry resentments by undue chastisements and] set yourself to his ruin.

¹⁹A man of great wrath shall suffer the penalty; for if you deliver him [from the consequences], he will [feel free to] cause you to do it again.

²⁰Hear counsel, receive instruction, and accept correction, that you may be wise in the time to come.

²¹Many plans are in a man's mind, but it is the Lord's purpose for him that will stand.

²²That which is desired in a man is loyalty and kindness [and his glory and delight are his giving], but a poor man is better than a liar.

²³The reverent, worshipful fear of the Lord leads to life, and he who has it rests satisfied; he cannot be visited with [actual] evil.

²⁴The sluggard buries his hand in the dish, and will not so much as bring it to his mouth again.

²⁵Strike a scoffer, and the simple will learn prudence; reprove a man of understanding, and he will increase in knowledge.

²⁶He who does violence to his father and chases away his mother is a son who causes shame and brings reproach.

²⁷Cease, my son, to hear instruction only to ignore it and stray from the words of knowledge.

²⁸A worthless witness scoffs at justice, and the mouth of the wicked swallows iniquity.

²⁹Judgments are prepared for scoffers, and stripes for the backs of [self-confident] fools.

PROVERBS 20

¹WINE IS a mocker, strong drink a riotous brawler; and whoever errs or reels because of it is not wise.

²The terror of a king is as the roaring of a lion; whoever provokes him to anger or angers himself against him sins against his own life.

³It is an honor for a man to cease from strife and keep aloof from it, but every fool will quarrel.

⁴The sluggard does not plow when winter sets in; therefore he begs in harvest and has nothing.

⁵Counsel in the heart of man is like water in a deep well, but a man of understanding draws it out.

⁶Many a man proclaims his own loving-kindness and goodness, but a faithful man who can find?

⁷The righteous man walks in his integrity; blessed (happy, fortunate, enviable) are his children after him.

⁸A king who sits on the throne of judgment winnows out all evil [like chaff] with his eyes.

⁹Who can say, I have made my heart clean, I am pure from my sin?

¹⁰Diverse weights [one for buying and another for selling] and diverse measures--both of them are exceedingly offensive and abhorrent to the Lord.

¹¹Even a child is known by his acts, whether [or not] what he does is pure and right.

¹²The hearing ear and the seeing eye--the Lord has made both of them.

¹³Love not sleep, lest you come to poverty; open your eyes and you will be satisfied with bread.

¹⁴It is worthless, it is worthless! says the buyer; but when he goes his way, then he boasts [about his bargain].

¹⁵There is gold, and a multitude of pearls, but the lips of knowledge are a vase of preciousness [the most precious of all].

¹⁶[The judge tells the creditor] Take the garment of one who is security for a stranger; and hold him in pledge when he is security for foreigners.

¹⁷Food gained by deceit is sweet to a man, but afterward his mouth will be filled with gravel.

¹⁸Purposes and plans are established by counsel; and [only] with good advice make or carry on war.

¹⁹He who goes about as a talebearer reveals secrets; therefore associate not with him who talks too freely.

²⁰Whoever curses his father or his mother, his lamp shall be put out in complete darkness.

²¹An inheritance hastily gotten [by greedy, unjust means] at the beginning, in the end it will not be blessed.

²²Do not say, I will repay evil; wait [expectantly] for the Lord, and He will rescue you.

²³Diverse and deceitful weights are shamefully vile and abhorrent to the Lord, and false scales are not good.

²⁴Man's steps are ordered by the Lord. How then can a man understand his way?

²⁵It is a snare to a man to utter a vow [of consecration] rashly and [not until] afterward inquire [whether he can fulfill it].

²⁶A wise king winnows out the wicked [from among the good] and brings the threshing wheel over them [to separate the chaff from the grain].

²⁷The spirit of man [that factor in human personality which proceeds immediately from God] is the lamp of the Lord, searching all his innermost parts.

²⁸Loving-kindness and mercy, truth and faithfulness, preserve the king, and his throne is upheld by [the people's] loyalty.

²⁹The glory of young men is their strength, and the beauty of old men is their gray head [suggesting wisdom and experience].

³⁰Blows that wound cleanse away evil, and strokes [for correction] reach to the innermost parts.

PROVERBS 21

¹THE KING'S heart is in the hand of the Lord, as are the watercourses; He turns it whichever way He wills.

²Every way of a man is right in his own eyes, but the Lord weighs and tries the hearts.

³To do righteousness and justice is more acceptable to the Lord than sacrifice.

⁴Haughtiness of eyes and a proud heart, even the tillage of the wicked or the lamp [of joy] to them [whatever it may be], are sin [in the eyes of God].

⁵The thoughts of the [steadily] diligent tend only to plenteousness, but everyone who is impatient and hasty hastens only to want.

⁶Securing treasures by a lying tongue is a vapor driven to and fro; those who seek them seek death.

⁷The violence of the wicked shall sweep them away, because they refuse to do justice.

⁸The way of the guilty is exceedingly crooked, but as for the pure, his work is right and his conduct is straight.

⁹It is better to dwell in a corner of the housetop [on the flat oriental roof, exposed to all kinds of weather] than in a house shared with a nagging, quarrelsome, and faultfinding woman.

¹⁰The soul or life of the wicked craves and seeks evil; his neighbor finds no favor in his eyes.

¹¹When the scoffer is punished, the fool gets a lesson in being wise; but men of [godly] Wisdom and good sense learn by being instructed.

¹²The [uncompromisingly] righteous man considers well the house of the wicked--how the wicked are cast down to ruin.

¹³Whoever stops his ears at the cry of the poor will cry out himself and not be heard.

¹⁴A gift in secret pacifies and turns away anger, and a bribe in the lap, strong wrath.

¹⁵When justice is done, it is a joy to the righteous (the upright, in right standing with God), but to the evildoers it is dismay, calamity, and ruin.

¹⁶A man who wanders out of the way of understanding shall abide in the congregation of the spirits (of the dead).

¹⁷He who loves pleasure will be a poor man; he who loves wine and oil will not be rich.

¹⁸The wicked become a ransom for the [uncompromisingly] righteous, and the treacherous for the upright [because the wicked themselves fall into the traps and pits they have dug for the good].

¹⁹It is better to dwell in a desert land than with a contentious woman and with vexation.

²⁰There are precious treasures and oil in the dwelling of the wise, but a self-confident and foolish man swallows it up and wastes it.

²¹He who earnestly seeks after and craves righteousness, mercy, and loving-kindness will find life in addition to righteousness (uprightness and right standing with God) and honor.

²²A wise man scales the city walls of the mighty and brings down the stronghold in which they trust.

²³He who guards his mouth and his tongue keeps himself from troubles.

²⁴The proud and haughty man--Scoffer is his name--deals and acts with overbearing pride.

²⁵The desire of the slothful kills him, for his hands refuse to labor.

²⁶He covets greedily all the day long, but the [uncompromisingly] righteous gives and does not withhold.

²⁷The sacrifice of the wicked is exceedingly disgusting and abhorrent [to the Lord]--how much more when he brings it with evil intention?

²⁸A false witness will perish, but the word of a man who hears attentively will endure and go unchallenged.

²⁹A wicked man puts on the bold, unfeeling face [of guilt], but as for the upright, he considers, directs, and establishes his way [with the confidence of integrity].

³⁰There is no [human] wisdom or understanding or counsel [that can prevail] against the Lord.

³¹The horse is prepared for the day of battle, but deliverance and victory are of the Lord.

PROVERBS 22

¹A GOOD name is rather to be chosen than great riches, and loving favor rather than silver and gold.

²The rich and poor meet together; the Lord is the Maker of them all.

³A prudent man sees the evil and hides himself, but the simple pass on and are punished [with suffering].

⁴The reward of humility and the reverent and worshipful fear of the Lord is riches and honor and life.

⁵Thorns and snares are in the way of the obstinate and willful; he who guards himself will be far from them.

⁶Train up a child in the way he should go [and in keeping with his individual gift or bent], and when he is old he will not depart from it.

⁷The rich rule over the poor, and the borrower is servant to the lender.

⁸He who sows iniquity will reap calamity and futility, and the rod of his wrath [with which he smites others] will fail.

⁹He who has a bountiful eye shall be blessed, for he gives of his bread to the poor.

¹⁰Drive out the scoffer, and contention will go out; yes, strife and abuse will cease.

¹¹He who loves purity and the pure in heart and who is gracious in speech--because of the grace of his lips will he have the king for his friend.

¹²The eyes of the Lord keep guard over knowledge and him who has it, but He overthrows the words of the treacherous.

¹³The sluggard says, There is a lion outside! I shall be slain in the streets!

¹⁴The mouth of a loose woman is a deep pit [for ensnaring wild animals]; he with whom the Lord is indignant and who is abhorrent to Him will fall into it.

¹⁵Foolishness is bound up in the heart of a child, but the rod of discipline will drive it far from him.

¹⁶He who oppresses the poor to get gain for himself and he who gives to the rich--both will surely come to want.

¹⁷Listen (consent and submit) to the words of the wise, and apply your mind to my knowledge;

¹⁸For it will be pleasant if you keep them in your mind [believing them]; your lips will be accustomed to [confessing] them.

¹⁹So that your trust (belief, reliance, support, and confidence) may be in the Lord, I have made known these things to you today, even to you.

²⁰Have I not written to you [long ago] excellent things in counsels and knowledge,

²¹To make you know the certainty of the words of truth, that you may give a true answer to those who sent you?

²²Rob not the poor [being tempted by their helplessness], neither oppress the afflicted at the gate [where the city court is held],

²³For the Lord will plead their cause and deprive of life those who deprive [the poor or afflicted].

²⁴Make no friendships with a man given to anger, and with a wrathful man do not associate,

²⁵Lest you learn his ways and get yourself into a snare.

²⁶Be not one of those who strike hands and pledge themselves, or of those who become security for another's debts.

²⁷If you have nothing with which to pay, why should he take your bed from under you?

²⁸Remove not the ancient landmark which your fathers have set up.

²⁹Do you see a man diligent and skillful in his business? He will stand before kings; he will not stand before obscure men.

PROVERBS 23

¹WHEN YOU sit down to eat with a ruler, consider who and what are before you;

²For you will put a knife to your throat if you are a man given to desire.

³Be not desirous of his dainties, for it is deceitful food [offered with questionable motives].

⁴Weary not yourself to be rich; cease from your own [human] wisdom.

⁵Will you set your eyes upon wealth, when [suddenly] it is gone? For riches certainly make themselves wings, like an eagle that flies toward the heavens.

⁶Eat not the bread of him who has a hard, grudging, and envious eye, neither desire his dainty foods;

⁷For as he thinks in his heart, so is he. As one who reckons, he says to you, eat and drink, yet his heart is not with you [but is grudging the cost].

⁸The morsel which you have eaten you will vomit up, and your complimentary words will be wasted.

⁹Speak not in the ears of a [self-confident] fool, for he will despise the [godly] Wisdom of your words.

¹⁰Remove not the ancient landmark and enter not into the fields of the fatherless,

¹¹For their Redeemer is mighty; He will plead their cause against you.

¹²Apply your mind to instruction and correction and your ears to words of knowledge.

¹³Withhold not discipline from the child; for if you strike and punish him with the [reedlike] rod, he will not die.

[14]You shall whip him with the rod and deliver his life from death.

[15]My son, if your heart is wise, my heart will be glad, even mine;

[16]Yes, my heart will rejoice when your lips speak right things.

[17]Let not your heart envy sinners, but continue in the reverent and worshipful fear of the Lord all the day long.

[18]For surely there is a latter end [a future and a reward], and your hope and expectation shall not be cut off.

[19]Hear, my son, and be wise, and direct your mind in the way [of the Lord].

[20]Do not associate with winebibbers; be not among them nor among gluttonous eaters of meat,

[21]For the drunkard and the glutton shall come to poverty, and drowsiness shall clothe a man with rags.

[22]Hearken to your father, who begot you, and despise not your mother when she is old.

[23]Buy the truth and sell it not; not only that, but also get discernment and judgment, instruction and understanding.

[24]The father of the [uncompromisingly] righteous (the upright, in right standing with God) shall greatly rejoice, and he who becomes the father of a wise child shall have joy in him.

[25]Let your father and your mother be glad, and let her who bore you rejoice.

[26]My son, give me your heart and let your eyes observe and delight in my ways,

[27]For a harlot is a deep ditch, and a loose woman is a narrow pit.

[28]She also lies in wait as a robber or as one waits for prey, and she increases the treacherous among men.

[29]Who has woe? Who has sorrow? Who has strife? Who has complaining? Who has wounds without cause? Who has redness and dimness of eyes?

[30]Those who tarry long at the wine, those who go to seek and try mixed wine.

[31]Do not look at wine when it is red, when it sparkles in the wineglass, when it goes down smoothly.

[32]At the last it bites like a serpent and stings like an adder.

[33][Under the influence of wine] your eyes will behold strange things [and loose women] and your mind will utter things turned the wrong way [untrue, incorrect, and petulant].

³⁴Yes, you will be [as unsteady] as he who lies down in the midst of the sea, and [as open to disaster] as he who lies upon the top of a mast.

³⁵You will say, They struck me, but I was not hurt! They beat me [as with a hammer], but I did not feel it! When shall I awake? I will crave and seek more wine again [and escape reality].

PROVERBS 24

¹BE NOT envious of evil men, nor desire to be with them;

²For their minds plot oppression and devise violence, and their lips talk of causing trouble and vexation.

³Through skillful and godly Wisdom is a house (a life, a home, a family) built, and by understanding it is established [on a sound and good foundation],

⁴And by knowledge shall its chambers [of every area] be filled with all precious and pleasant riches.

⁵A wise man is strong and is better than a strong man, and a man of knowledge increases and strengthens his power;

⁶For by wise counsel you can wage your war, and in an abundance of counselors there is victory and safety.

⁷Wisdom is too high for a fool; he opens not his mouth in the gate [where city's rulers sit in judgment].

⁸He who plans to do evil will be called a mischief-maker.

⁹The plans of the foolish and the thought of foolishness are sin, and the scoffer is an abomination to men.

¹⁰If you faint in the day of adversity, your strength is small.

¹¹Deliver those who are drawn away to death, and those who totter to the slaughter, hold them back [from their doom].

¹²If you [profess ignorance and] say, Behold, we did not know this, does not He Who weighs and ponders the heart perceive and consider it? And He Who guards your life, does not He know it? And shall not He render to [you and] every man according to his works?

¹³My son, eat honey, because it is good, and the drippings of the honeycomb are sweet to your taste.

¹⁴So shall you know skillful and godly Wisdom to be thus to your life; if you find it, then shall there be a future and a reward, and your hope and expectation shall not be cut off.

[15]Lie not in wait as a wicked man against the dwelling of the [uncompromisingly] righteous (the upright, in right standing with God); destroy not his resting-place;

[16]For a righteous man falls seven times and rises again, but the wicked are overthrown by calamity.

[17]Rejoice not when your enemy falls, and let not your heart be glad when he stumbles or is overthrown,

[18]Lest the Lord see it and it be evil in His eyes and displease Him, and He turn away His wrath from him [to expend it upon you, the worse offender].

[19]Fret not because of evildoers, neither be envious of the wicked,

[20]For there shall be no reward for the evil man; the lamp of the wicked shall be put out.

[21]My son, [reverently] fear the Lord and the king, and do not associate with those who are given to change [of allegiance, and are revolutionary],

[22]For their calamity shall rise suddenly, and who knows the punishment and ruin which both [the Lord and the king] will bring upon [the rebellious]?

[23]These also are sayings of the wise: To discriminate and show partiality, having respect of persons in judging, is not good.

[24]He who says to the wicked, You are righteous and innocent-- peoples will curse him, nations will defy and abhor him.

[25]But to those [upright judges] who rebuke the wicked, it will go well with them and they will find delight, and a good blessing will be upon them.

[26]He kisses the lips [and wins the hearts of men] who give a right answer.

[27][Put first things first.] Prepare your work outside and get it ready for yourself in the field; and afterward build your house and establish a home.

[28]Be not a witness against your neighbor without cause, and deceive not with your lips.

[29]Say not, I will do to him as he has done to me; I will pay the man back for his deed.

[30]I went by the field of the lazy man, and by the vineyard of the man void of understanding;

³¹And, behold, it was all grown over with thorns, and nettles were covering its face, and its stone wall was broken down.

³²Then I beheld and considered it well; I looked and received instruction.

³³Yet a little sleep, a little slumber, a little folding of the hands to sleep--

³⁴So shall your poverty come as a robber, and your want as an armed man.

PROVERBS 25

¹THESE ARE also the proverbs of Solomon, which the men of Hezekiah king of Judah copied:

²It is the glory of God to conceal a thing, but the glory of kings is to search out a thing.

³As the heavens for height and the earth for depth, so the hearts and minds of kings are unsearchable.

⁴Take away the dross from the silver, and there shall come forth [the material for] a vessel for the silversmith [to work up].

⁵Take away the wicked from before the king, and his throne will be established in righteousness (moral and spiritual rectitude in every area and relation).

⁶Be not forward (self-assertive and boastfully ambitious) in the presence of the king, and stand not in the place of great men;

⁷For better it is that it should be said to you, Come up here, than that you should be put lower in the presence of the prince, whose eyes have seen you.

⁸Rush not forth soon to quarrel [before magistrates or elsewhere], lest you know not what to do in the end when your neighbor has put you to shame.

⁹Argue your cause with your neighbor himself; discover not and disclose not another's secret,

¹⁰Lest he who hears you revile you and bring shame upon you and your ill repute have no end.

¹¹A word fitly spoken and in due season is like apples of gold in settings of silver.

¹²Like an earring or nose ring of gold or an ornament of fine gold is a wise reprover to an ear that listens and obeys.

¹³Like the cold of snow [brought from the mountains] in the time of harvest, so is a faithful messenger to those who send him; for he refreshes the life of his masters.

¹⁴Whoever falsely boasts of gifts [he does not give] is like clouds and wind without rain.

¹⁵By long forbearance and calmness of spirit a judge or ruler is persuaded, and soft speech breaks down the most bonelike resistance.

¹⁶Have you found [pleasure sweet like] honey? Eat only as much as is sufficient for you, lest, being filled with it, you vomit it.

¹⁷Let your foot seldom be in your neighbor's house, lest he become tired of you and hate you.

¹⁸A man who bears false witness against his neighbor is like a heavy sledgehammer and a sword and a sharp arrow.

¹⁹Confidence in an unfaithful man in time of trouble is like a broken tooth or a foot out of joint.

²⁰He who sings songs to a heavy heart is like him who lays off a garment in cold weather and like vinegar upon soda.

²¹If your enemy is hungry, give him bread to eat; and if he is thirsty, give him water to drink;

²²For in doing so, you will heap coals of fire upon his head, and the Lord will reward you.

²³The north wind brings forth rain; so does a backbiting tongue bring forth an angry countenance.

²⁴It is better to dwell in the corner of the housetop than to share a house with a disagreeing, quarrelsome, and scolding woman.

²⁵Like cold water to a thirsty soul, so is good news from a far [home] country.

²⁶Like a muddied fountain and a polluted spring is a righteous man who yields, falls down, and compromises his integrity before the wicked.

²⁷It is not good to eat much honey; so for men to seek glory, their own glory, causes suffering and is not glory.

²⁸He who has no rule over his own spirit is like a city that is broken down and without walls.

PROVERBS 26

¹LIKE SNOW in summer and like rain in harvest, so honor is not fitting for a [self-confident] fool.

²Like the sparrow in her wandering, like the swallow in her flying, so the causeless curse does not alight.

³A whip for the horse, a bridle for the donkey, and a [straight, slender] rod for the backs of [self-confident] fools.

⁴Answer not a [self-confident] fool according to his folly, lest you also be like him.

⁵Answer a [self-confident] fool according to his folly, lest he be wise in his own eyes and conceit.

⁶He who sends a message by the hand of a [a]fool cuts off the feet [of satisfactory delivery] and drinks the damage.

⁷Like the legs of a lame man which hang loose, so is a parable in the mouth of a fool.

⁸Like he who binds a stone in a sling, so is he who gives honor to a [self-confident] fool.

⁹Like a thorn that goes [without being felt] into the hand of a drunken man, so is a proverb in the mouth of a [self-confident] fool.

¹⁰[But] like an archer who wounds all, so is he who hires a fool or chance passers-by.

¹¹As a dog returns to his vomit, so a fool returns to his folly.

¹²Do you see a man wise in his own eyes and conceit? There is more hope for a [self-confident] fool than for him.

¹³The sluggard says, There is a lion in the way! A lion is in the streets!

¹⁴As the door turns on its hinges, so does the lazy man [move not from his place] upon his bed.

¹⁵The slothful and self-indulgent buries his hand in his bosom; it distresses and wearies him to bring it again to his mouth.

¹⁶The sluggard is wiser in his own eyes and conceit than seven men who can render a reason and answer discreetly.

¹⁷He who, passing by, stops to meddle with strife that is none of his business is like one who takes a dog by the ears.

¹⁸Like a madman who casts firebrands, arrows, and death,

¹⁹So is the man who deceives his neighbor and then says, Was I not joking?

²⁰For lack of wood the fire goes out, and where there is no whisperer, contention ceases.

²¹As coals are to hot embers and as wood to fire, so is a quarrelsome man to inflame strife.

²²The words of a whisperer or slanderer are like dainty morsels or words of sport [to some, but to others are like deadly wounds]; and they go down into the innermost parts of the body [or of the victim's nature].

²³Burning lips [uttering insincere words of love] and a wicked heart are like an earthen vessel covered with the scum thrown off from molten silver [making it appear to be solid silver].

²⁴He who hates pretends with his lips, but stores up deceit within himself.

²⁵When he speaks kindly, do not trust him, for seven abominations are in his heart.

²⁶Though his hatred covers itself with guile, his wickedness shall be shown openly before the assembly.

²⁷Whoever digs a pit [for another man's feet] shall fall into it himself, and he who rolls a stone [up a height to do mischief], it will return upon him.

²⁸A lying tongue hates those it wounds and crushes, and a flattering mouth works ruin.

PROVERBS 27

¹DO NOT boast of [yourself and] tomorrow, for you know not what a day may bring forth.

²Let another man praise you, and not your own mouth; a stranger, and not your own lips.

³Stone is heavy and sand weighty, but a fool's [unreasoning] wrath is heavier and more intolerable than both of them.

⁴Wrath is cruel and anger is an overwhelming flood, but who is able to stand before jealousy?

⁵Open rebuke is better than love that is hidden.

⁶Faithful are the wounds of a friend, but the kisses of an enemy are lavish and deceitful.

⁷He who is satiated [with sensual pleasures] loathes and treads underfoot a honeycomb, but to the hungry soul every bitter thing is sweet.

⁸Like a bird that wanders from her nest, so is a man who strays from his home.

⁹Oil and perfume rejoice the heart; so does the sweetness of a friend's counsel that comes from the heart.

¹⁰Your own friend and your father's friend, forsake them not; neither go to your brother's house in the day of your calamity. Better is a neighbor who is near [in spirit] than a brother who is far off [in heart].

¹¹My son, be wise, and make my heart glad, that I may answer him who reproaches me [as having failed in my parental duty].

¹²A prudent man sees the evil and hides himself, but the simple pass on and are punished [with suffering].

¹³[The judge tells the creditor] Take the garment of one who is security for a stranger; and hold him in pledge when he is security for foreigners.

¹⁴The flatterer who loudly praises and glorifies his neighbor, rising early in the morning, it shall be counted as cursing him [for he will be suspected of sinister purposes].

¹⁵A continual dripping on a day of violent showers and a contentious woman are alike;

¹⁶Whoever attempts to restrain [a contentious woman] might as well try to stop the wind--his right hand encounters oil [and she slips through his fingers].

¹⁷Iron sharpens iron; so a man sharpens the countenance of his friend [to show rage or worthy purpose].

¹⁸Whoever tends the fig tree shall eat its fruit; so he who patiently and faithfully guards and heeds his master shall be honored.

¹⁹As in water face answers to and reflects face, so the heart of man to man.

²⁰Sheol (the place of the dead) and Abaddon (the place of destruction) are never satisfied; so [the lust of] the eyes of man is never satisfied.

²¹As the refining pot for silver and the furnace for gold [bring forth all the impurities of the metal], so let a man be in his trial of praise [ridding himself of all that is base or insincere; for a man is judged by what he praises and of what he boasts].

²²Even though like grain you should pound a fool in a mortar with a pestle, yet will not his foolishness depart from him.

²³Be diligent to know the state of your flocks, and look well to your herds;

²⁴For riches are not forever; does a crown endure to all generations?

²⁵When the hay is gone, the tender grass shows itself, and herbs of the mountain are gathered in,

²⁶The lambs will be for your clothing, and the goats [will furnish you] the price of a field.

²⁷And there will be goats' milk enough for your food, for the food of your household, and for the maintenance of your maids.

PROVERBS 28

¹THE WICKED flee when no man pursues them, but the righteous are bold as a lion.

²When a land transgresses, it has many rulers, but when the ruler is a man of discernment, understanding, and knowledge, its stability will long continue.

³A poor man who oppresses the poor is like a sweeping rain which leaves no food [plundering them of their last morsels].

⁴Those who forsake the law [of God and man] praise the wicked, but those who keep the law [of God and man] contend with them.

⁵Evil men do not understand justice, but they who crave and seek the Lord understand it fully.

⁶Better is the poor man who walks in his integrity than he who willfully goes in double and wrong ways, though he is rich.

⁷Whoever keeps the law [of God and man] is a wise son, but he who is a companion of gluttons and the carousing, self-indulgent, and extravagant shames his father.

⁸He who by charging excessive interest and who by unjust efforts to get gain increases his material possession gathers it for him [to spend] who is kind and generous to the poor.

⁹He who turns away his ear from hearing the law [of God and man], even his prayer is an abomination, hateful and revolting [to God].

¹⁰Whoever leads the upright astray into an evil way, he will himself fall into his own pit, but the blameless will have a goodly inheritance.

¹¹The rich man is wise in his own eyes and conceit, but the poor man who has understanding will find him out.